A Buyer's Guide To Business Coaching

Clare Moore and Brian Wishart

Business Jigsaw Press
www.businessjigsaw.com

First published in Great Britain in 2008

ISBN 978–0–9553660–2–4

A CIP catalogue record for this book is available from the British Library.

Cover design and diagrams by Sandy Hamilton of Hamilton Designs
Illustrations by Iain Mackintosh
Cartoons by Jim Barker

Typeset by Word4Word
Printed and bound in Great Britain by Lightning Source Ltd

What others are saying about

A Buyers Guide to Business Coaching

> *"An invaluable and timely guide for all business people who need to get to grips quickly with how coaching builds high performance in your organisation."* **– Howard Nelson, Transformation Executive, IBM Corporation**

> *"It is excellent to find a practical book that actually sees the importance of the business context in providing value from coaching and not a simple focus on the individual."* **– Mike Conway, VP Resourcing and Development at Royal Dutch Shell**

> *"A pragmatic book that shows that coaching needn't be fluffy . . . but can be both measured and transformational."* **– Sean Weafer, Founder member and Honorary Vice President of the Association for Coaching, London**

> *"In a frantic world where coaching is growing exponentially this is a very timely guide to help busy people get to grips with what they need to know to achieve value from coaching."* **– Ian Hunter, Founding Partner of Orion Partners, and author of *The Seven Steps of Executive Coaching***

> *"This highly useful book provides a step by step guide to choosing and hiring coaches, highlighting best practice and pitfalls and exploding a few myths along the way. Supported by a variety of very pertinent case histories, the text is easy to follow, clear and practical. A valuable addition to the HR executive's library, the book will also provide helpful information to coaches wishing to increase their activities in the corporate sector."* **– Carol Wilson, MD Performance Coach Training Ltd, Head of Accreditation Association for Coaching**

Acknowledgements

The writing of a book is a great way to reconnect to long standing and trusted friends and colleagues and to make some new ones along the way. There are, therefore, many people who have contributed to the thoughts and ideas that make up this book.

The authors would like to thank them all for their help and advice and in doing so hope they have remembered to acknowledge everyone that played a part.

Elina Koussis, Sophy Pern, Marianne Tracy, Douglas Young and Murli Nathan, for all their help with ideas and challenges in the preparation of the text.

Chris Pilling, Ian Hunter, David Nicholson, Mike Conway, Andrew Waller, Howard Nelson, Sean Weafer, Andy Smith and Carol Wilson for their insights, helpful comments and supportive quotes.

Deirdre McDonald, Peter Honey, Paul Barker, Alice Hurley, Liz Macann, Sally Bonneywell and Tim Haynes for case studies and permission to use their work.

Judy Fulton, Alison Smith and Emma Bell for editing, proof reading and helping to make sure it all makes sense.

Sandy Hamilton, Iain McIntosh and Jim Barker for the cover design, illustrations and cartoons.

Sue and the team at Word4Word for the layout, proof reading and general advice in getting the book to print.

Table of contents

Foreword

It is often only with hindsight that we see where a trend started to emerge. In the case of business coaching, it is perhaps a more predictable type of trend. Ten years ago, business futurologists like Tom Peters and Charles Handy were evangelising about the personalisation of services, the feminisation of the workplace (and consumer markets) and the death of traditional careers to be replaced by a project-to-project existence without the huge support infrastructures so common in large organisations then.

Since then, we have seen a strong shift away from command and control working cultures to a coaching style in all sorts of industries. As product and service personalisation has developed with one-to-one marketing, so have the internal services such as management development. As organisations have re-organised and de-layered, managers and leaders are expected to take on broader roles and get up to speed much faster. Many talented and experienced executives have jumped out of their corporate worlds into a different working pattern, creating a new lifestyle of "portfolio working."

In light of these trends, the rapid growth of one-to-one executive coaching should not be surprising. The market is still in a growth phase, it is largely unregulated and suffers all of the weaknesses one might therefore expect:

➡ an element of untrained yet influential and maybe even misguided individuals potentially giving the profession a bad name

➡ a lack of clear standards by which a buyer might judge the quality of the service

➡ a wide variation in prices

➡ an element of "flavour of the month" advocacy by some clients

Despite these hazards, organisations can find great benefits by investing properly in the right individuals with the right back up, on the right terms. Leading a team, going through change or just surviving in the complexity of modern day business is challenging and the benefits of a coach are many and often profound.

The publication of this book is therefore timely, as it offers some very sound advice to anyone who thinks they could be getting the benefits of coaching and who wants to avoid the potential pitfalls. To those of us who are not knee-deep in Human Resources theory and practice, but who want to support our teams to a higher level of performance, it provides a map through the various types of coaching; a method to select the right match for our needs and some excellent guidance for putting together the contract on terms that suit our needs. The final chapter on future trends is also stimulating food for thought when planning the next steps for the team.

As the coaching market matures, I see a lot of books and reports talking about coaching. Most are written by coaches or academics, and don't offer much in the way of practical advice. At last, this is a guide to coaching that actually helps drive value to the business. Brian Wishart and Clare Moore have used their unique perspective as clients, business managers, HR professionals and executive coaches to show how to work our investment hard.

If you are looking for sound pragmatic advice on coaching, save yourself some time and money and read this book.

Chris Pilling
CEO First Direct

Introduction

Our message is simple. Coaching should be treated as a business resource to be invested in wisely. The book you are reading now was designed to be, above all, useful; a practical guide for people buying coaching. We have tried to set a no-nonsense, business tone and to include case studies and real life stories that bring the points to life in a meaningful way.

So how did it come about? We met at the Association for Coaching Conference in Edinburgh and in true networking style, exchanged contact details and agreed to meet again.

We had a lot in common – we had both worked in large corporate organisations, we had both been involved in organisational development and experienced the benefits of a great business coach. We had both left that world to return to Scotland and set up our own businesses and we were both successfully combining consultancy with business coaching.

At a subsequent lunch meeting, we hatched a plot to write an unusual coaching book. There were plenty of books out there about how to become a coach, various coaching methodologies and models and even how to be your own coach. This book would be for the **buyers**, rather than the coach or the client. Although, as coaches, we realise how useful it is for coaches to be able to step into their client's shoes none of the coaching books we had read seemed to cover the needs of the people who were spending the money. We felt that having seen all three sides of the triangle, we were well placed to research best practice and present a useful and practical guide.

We agreed that all of the signs in the market were that coaching was growing as a discipline. A recent survey of senior managers in UK private and public sector organisations found that one-to-one confidential coaching is now taking a substantial proportion of organisations' training budgets. The increasing trend in the popularity of coaching for senior executives is given particular mention within the survey.

"Given the flexibility of coaching in addressing specific and individual development needs, it seems that a transition in the status of coaching is occurring, as it becomes a necessity and not just a nicety." – QED Consulting Survey, June 2006

HR consultancies, outplacement firms and management consultancies all seem to be beefing up their coaching divisions, ready to supply the burgeoning market.

Alongside the larger organisations, legions of newly qualified business coaches are entering the market every month. Coaching is here to stay and more and more organisations need help to navigate their way through the potential minefields of finding, contracting with, managing and removing coaches.

While no coach would like to be thought of as a commodity, we believe there is too much subjectivity in the decision-making process and too much money wasted as a result.

In designing the structure of the book, we thought about the questions the buyer is faced with: What type of coaching might I need, where do I find the right coach and how do I know I'm getting the best value I can?

You may have used coaching before, or just be aware of it as a possible way to deal with improving performance at work. There are many myths and beliefs about coaching that might set unrealistic expectations: It's a panacea for any problem; it will make you into Terry Leahy, CEO, Tesco, after three sessions; every session is a life changing experience; it's unaffordable, ineffective and un-measurable; only for high fliers; only for people with problems; coaches have to be grey haired and highly qualified psychologists.

In the book, we aim to dispel the myths and provide clear and practical guidance about when to engage the services of a coach, how to approach the contract, which pricing model to use, how to prepare the client and their line manager and evaluate the arrangement, so that your organisation is getting the best value possible. We also look to the future and consider the trends in the coaching marketplace, to give you food for thought about where you could steer your strategy for coaching going forward.

We hope you enjoy the book and as a result of reading it, gain the full benefits of what we believe can be a hugely powerful development tool.

Clare Moore
Brian Wishart

Chapter 1 – Good reasons to use coaching

Why are you thinking about coaching?

"The Operations manager has had his own coach for six months now and seems to be really getting his act together. I'm wondering if I should get one."

"The HR Manager says he wants me to take part in this trial the firm is doing of a new course and it means I'd have to spend half a day a month with a coach. I can't afford to give up half a day a month, don't they realise how much work I've got on? I think it will be a complete waste of time and money."

"I met this woman last week who does executive coaching and she seemed quite switched on. I wouldn't mind trying her out, it might help me deal with this new project."

"I've got to do something with the managers in this team to move them up a level. A one-off training course isn't going to do it. Coaching might be the answer."

Whatever your reasons for thinking about coaching, you have picked up a book that will help you work out exactly what you need and how to go about finding it.

In this chapter we will look at:

➡ Some common reasons to use coaching

➡ Considering the alternatives

➡ I need something but do I need a coach?

➡ Could you be uncoachable?

➡ What if they leave?

Some common reasons to use coaching

"Executives should seek coaching when they feel that a change in behaviour – either for themselves or their team members – can make a significant difference in the long term success of the organisation." Marshall Goldsmith,

a high profile coach and author of 18 books including *The Leader of the Future*.

These are some of the common reasons for looking for a business coach:

1. Promotion to a new job/on-boarding

This is such a common trigger that many coaching firms have designed intensive packages around the "First 100 days" in a new role. An external, unbiased voice can be particularly useful when you have been promoted from within your peer group.

In cases where a technical specialist is promoted into a management role for the first time they may find that the skills that got them this far are not sufficient to succeed in the new arena. A coach can help the new manager identify the areas that need to be developed or sharpened up and focus on a plan to achieve that.

2. Stretching assignments

In organisations that are flatter than ever, it is increasingly likely that high potential executives will be given challenging projects within a role, rather than moved up the ladder. These often involve working outside of the team or department they are used to, building new relationships and influencing colleagues and external contacts to deliver the project. Here a coach can help the manager step back from the task and help them develop influencing strategies and a more collaborative working style.

3. New challenges

Changes to the role are not the only triggers to new challenges within a job. Competitor activity, technological changes, social shifts and, especially in the public sector, Political movements can create significant areas of challenge.

Responding to these may require a different approach or a new level of thinking. Without any external prodding, it can be tempting to stick with what we know and never find the time to reach out for more creative strategies for dealing with these unfamiliar situations.

4. The team needs to work together better

Your team may be working well and achieving good results but that's not going to be enough. To move up a level, to reach higher targets or to deal with a new competitor or big product launch, the individuals need to pull together and improve their performance.

A team coach can work with each individual as well as the group as a whole to improve relationships, processes and alignment with team objectives.

5. When you are stuck

If you are feeling frustrated, burnt out, or that you are hitting your head against a brick wall, it may be time to reach for the phone. As in Michael's story below, perhaps balancing your workload has got to a point where you can't see the wood for the trees. In many cases, a relationship with a colleague is proving to be a blockage to achieving goals and tasks.

A coach can be the non-judgemental expert who can help you get to the fundamental cause of the issues and overcome the knotty problems that have got you trapped.

 ! Warning. You may uncover a need for counselling rather than coaching. Chapter 2 makes the distinction and talks about how to deal with this situation.

 I don't have time for a coach

Michael had a Programme Manager job for a government agency. He was juggling seven projects, five consultants, dozens of client relationships and his desk was an almighty mess.

His wife and children were planning on taking a holiday in ten days time and he was seriously considering sending them off without him.

At a full team Business Strategy meeting the day before, an organisational chart had been presented showing Michael as the lowest in the food chain, despite him having project budgets that dwarfed those on the top level.

He had been to see his GP a fortnight previously. She diagnosed high blood pressure and advised him to take steps to reduce his stress levels. He knew that even if he took the holiday, the volume and type of work was going to keep coming and if he didn't change his approach to it, he'd be back in the doctor's office before too long.

He had thought before about asking for a coach but rejected the idea, because he couldn't envisage freeing up the time to see them regularly.

His colleague, Dave, gently pointed out that things were not going to ease off any time soon and there was never a perfect time to take holidays. Michael thought about this on the way home (late) that night and booked his holiday. At the next meeting with his boss, he suggested that time with a coach might be useful.

Within three months, Michael had found a good coach and had spent regular time with him. Using Jim's help, he was able to see another way to manage his work that got the most important parts done and still kept his stress levels at a healthy level. He even found that he began to enjoy the challenge of the job again.

6. Smoothing the rough edges

You have a lot of the qualities needed for the project or the next job, but there are some areas where you need to change your ways. Sometimes called remedial coaching, this takes an area of concern and tries to tackle it. Whether it is the ability to influence without bulldozing or patronising others, the poor state of presentation skills, a blind spot around organisational politics or simply time management, some one-to-one coaching can be much more effective than a one off training course.

7. To embed new skills

After a training course or seminar where new knowledge and skills have been picked up, it is all too easy to slip back into the way we used to work. Regular coaching sessions that follow the training can ensure that the focus is maintained and the new skills put to good use.

8. Career management

No one cares more about your career than you do, even if there is someone in HR whose job it is to co-ordinate succession planning. Most of us are so tied up in the pressures of the current role that we rarely take the time to step back and work out which career path we'd really like to take.

Using a coach to help think this through, identifying the various options and planning out the steps to take can be very valuable. It also helps the organisation to retain their best people, as it helps to avoid the frustration of unrealistic expectations and the possible loss of that individual to another firm.

Considering the options

These are some of the triggers that may direct you to consider a coach to meet this learning need. There are, of course, many other ways to meet these needs. Elsewhere in the book, we will consider the clear advantages of coaching as well as other individual and organisational interventions.

Traditionally, development needs have been addressed using:

- Discussions with line managers
- Disciplinary action in cases of poor performance
- Technical or specialist training courses
- Mentoring (spending time learning from a more experienced colleague)
- Leadership or management development courses

Many organisations are using coaching as part of a wider programme of activities to develop and retain key staff.

Case study

In Scottish Power, the investment in coaching is part of exactly such a strategy. Deirdre McDonald outlined Scottish Power's Talent Management strategy at the Association for Coaching in Scotland Conference 2006. It sets out the way in which the organisation has decided to tackle recruiting, developing and retaining its people.

Scottish Power sees coaching as one of a range of tools available. Deirdre sees three key benefits: its individual approach, that it fits into schedules and it provides leverage to move the organisation towards a coaching culture.

It is one thing to identify the areas where some action is needed. It is quite another to find the best solution to take.

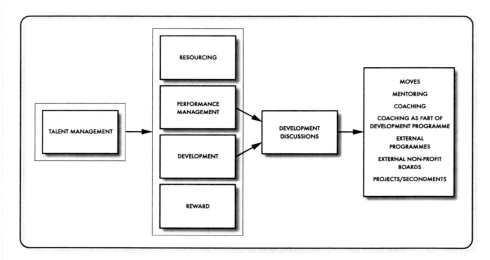

Figure 1. *Coaching for Individuals in Scottish Power*

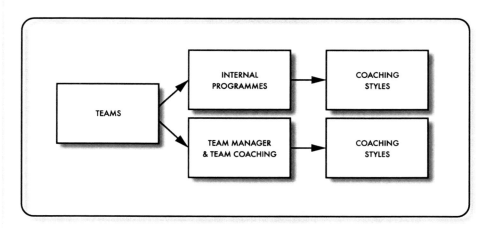

Figure 2. *Coaching for Teams in Scottish Power*

I need something, but do I need a coach?

If you have recognised the need to do something, through a conversation with your line manager or through personal development planning, there are many options to consider. A useful aid at this point is some work done by Jessica Jarvis of the Chartered Institute of Personnel Development.

This simple decision tree is designed to help in assessing whether coaching is the best approach to take (see Figure 3).

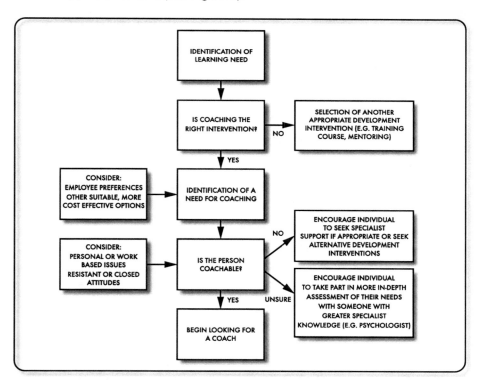

Figure 3. *Decision Tree: Is coaching an appropriate intervention?*

As this model identifies, there are some people who are not likely to benefit from coaching. Given the investment in time and money involved in a coaching programme, it is useful to find out what makes someone "uncoachable".

What makes you "uncoachable"?

Most business coaches agree that there are some people who are not going to gain very much from coaching. They are often the very people that HR managers or line managers would dearly love to bring in an external coach for. This may be because previous efforts to provide developmental feedback have ended up falling on deaf ears.

There are a number of useful questions to ask to find out whether a person might be "uncoachable":

1. Are you ready to change?
To get the benefit of coaching, it is important to be open to feedback and willing to make positive changes. For all sorts of reasons, an individual can have barriers up to receiving feedback or accepting that they could or should develop in any way.

This is where some people can surprise their colleagues by opening up to a coach when no one else seems able to get through.

2. Do you have a clear purpose and motivation to change?
As we discussed earlier in the chapter, coaching is most often demanded in times of change for the individual. Where the role is in a steady state and the individual is happy with their performance and results, not planning to expand the role or move to another position, there may be no burning need to use a coach. If the individual expects the coach to solves things for them and take no responsibility personally, then no long term advantage will be gained.

3. Are your needs deeper?
There are situations where the development area has roots in a deeper psychological need. In this case, a business coach may find themselves out of their depth and potentially treading on dangerous ground. For issues of depression or addiction, for example, consulting a doctor, trained psychologist or addiction counsellor is advised.

You may be looking for more of a spiritual direction, and again, a business coach may not be the best person to work with, although this is an area in which more and more business coaches are working.

4. Is it home or work that's the issue?
Business coaches often find that the discussion starts with job specific topics and frequently strays into issues of work/life balance. This is a grey area and some organisations are happy for both to be covered. Where a personal or family crisis is underway, a professional counsellor is a better option.

5. Could we see you in tribunal?
The CIPD advises against coaching where *"The individual continually engages in socially inappropriate behaviour, for example, bordering on sexual harassment, that is frequent and ingrained. Either the person in question will need long term*

intensive counselling or will be subject to the formal disciplinary process. As coaches can't refuse to testify against clients in any subsequent legal proceedings, it is also in the best interests of the employees themselves to have professional counsellors with whom to discuss problems in total confidentiality."

! Warning. At first glance, a manager may appear to be uncoachable. In some cases, given the opportunity to choose a suitable coach themselves, they can respond spectacularly well.

A client's story

Karen had worked in the financial services industry for 25 years, moving between five different firms. She had been accused of being arrogant, closed minded and difficult for most of her working life. She rejected this criticism and chose instead to dwell on her ability to get things done. She was frequently brought in to trouble-shoot, rescuing projects when others had failed.

When she was passed over for promotion, she asked for feedback. The HR Manager was convinced that Karen wouldn't accept the message that her failure to get on with colleagues had held her back. He told her it had been a close run thing and that Karen had just been pipped at the post by someone with more up to date skills.

Karen knew that the new boss, Jim, didn't have half the knowledge and expertise that she had built up in the firm and frequently voiced her frustration when he didn't immediately know the answer in meetings.

Jim was faced with a choice. He could move Karen on or try to turn her attitude around. Against the advice of his colleagues, he offered Karen a chance to join the Executive Coaching programme. He showed Karen a number of Coach CVs and she selected Bob because of his impressive experience in highly complex financial products. After satisfying herself that Bob was someone she could respect, on her terms, she gradually began to open up to him.

Bob was able to build a relationship of trust so that Karen would listen to the observations Bob had about the behaviour Karen had been displaying and experiencing in others. She recognised that her highly judgemental approach was damaging communication channels and reducing her effectiveness. After working with Bob over a six month period, Karen's colleagues found her much easier to work with. Jim and Karen agreed that she should represent the department on a major new project.

Having asked the "are you uncoachable" questions, and deciding that you could benefit from using a coach, there may be another hurdle to jump. A common fear among line managers is that their valued team member may end up leaving the team as a result of the coaching programme.

What if they leave?

One of the fears within organisations is that you spend a lot of money (See Chapter 4 for exactly how much) bringing in a coach, only to find that six months later, the high flier decides to leave the organisation. It later turns out that they have been using their coaching sessions to put their CV together and work on their exit strategy.

This is the same danger that organisations face with leadership development programmes in general. Any activity which asks the individual to stop and look at how they are living their life, how they are operating and how that matches with their own values and needs, runs the risk of spurring that person on to different things for them.

Most HR professionals take a philosophical view of such moves, believing that everyone gains. The individual was going to leave at some point anyway and has freed up the role for someone more motivated to do the job. In a coaching programme for twenty senior managers, if two or three leave earlier than expected, the "wasted" investment in coaching is more than offset by the increased contribution from those left behind.

CHAPTER SUMMARY

✓ **The Reasons Why People Use Coaching:** Coaching is typically used in times of change for the individual, whether triggered by a new role, new challenges within the role or to instigate change to tackle old problems in a new way.

✓ **Where Coaching Fits with Training and Mentoring:** When considering coaching, it is useful to consider the alternatives in light of the individuals' preferences and the team context. A decision tree is offered to help work through these elements.

✓ **Who Can Be Coached:** Only the coachable need apply. If you are open and ready to change, have challenges that a coach is trained to deal with and struggle to find time for week-long training courses, you could benefit from coaching. Sometimes those who seem to be uncoachable are actually those who can benefit most, given the right coach and the time to work together.

Chapter 2 – Deciding what type of coaching you need

Framing business coaching

This book addresses coaching in a business context. It looks to examine the value that a well chosen coach can add to the bottom line of a business performance, irrespective of the size or nature of that business. In a crowded coaching market a working definition or frame of reference is important. The potential buyer who wants to make an informed choice needs to be clear on what coaching territory they are in.

In this chapter we will look at:

➡ Framing business coaching

➡ What business coaching **is**

➡ What business coaching **is not**

➡ Coaching styles

➡ When to use a facilitative coaching style

➡ When to use a directive coaching style

What business coaching is

When considering a definition, where to start will be the first question. Apart from the Oxford Dictionary the most obvious place these days to look for a definition is of course the internet and "Wikipedia" or Google. It is somewhat distressing therefore that when you Google the word "coaching" you will unearth some ninety five pages describing everything from becoming the next world leader to useful tips for coaching goalkeepers in junior football. (This is also a bit depressing for authors of a coaching book where all the angles seem to have been covered in some form!)

The reason for the huge amount of coaching content on the web is that coaching has become very fashionable in both private and business life. It has expanded to cater for all tastes from life coaching film stars, sports and TV personalities through to business coaching for senior executives and on to the front line manager struggling with yet another organisational change. The number of coaches available is expanding rapidly as is the variety of types of coaching on offer.

 Fact

Coaching is an increasingly popular tool for supporting personal development. Just over six out of ten respondents in the CIPD Learning and development survey 2007 reported that they now use coaching in their organisations. Of these just over 50% say that their organisation sees coaching as a 'permanent style' of management and 73% of respondents expect to see coaching by line managers increase in the next few years.

A definition, along with some description of the boundaries is therefore important if we are going to help navigate this complexity for the benefit of business and personal success.

Some useful contemporary definitions of coaching in a business context include:

 "Unlocking a person's potential to maximise their own performance." – (Whitmore 1996)

"A process that enables learning and development to occur and thus performance to improve." – (Parsloe 1999)

"Primarily a short-term intervention aimed at performance improvement or developing a particular competence." – (Clutterbuck 2003)

The definitions have been selected from many available as they have a common underpinning theme of "performance improvement". But we go further in believing that coaching leads to the achievement of clear organisational objectives which, in turn, deliver improved business performance.

A working definition for the purposes of this book, defines business coaching as:

 "A formal engagement in which a skilled coach works with an individual in a series of conversations designed to establish and achieve clear goals that will result in improved business performance." – (Wishart and Moore 2007)

Although this attempts to be much more specific than some definitions, there are nevertheless a number of issues to be addressed in understanding what we mean by the terms "skilled coach", "conversation" and "improved business performance". Chapter 3 will cover how to find a suitably skilled coach and Chapters 4 to 6 outline the best ways to set up the coaching arrangement to deliver a measurably improved business performance. The type of conversation the coach and client will be having will largely be determined by the type of coaching programme you ask for. In this chapter, the various styles of coaching will be explained to help the buyer describe what is really needed.

In practice Business Coaching is about a series of regular conversations where the coach works in the best interests of the client towards goals that achieve improved business performance. The term is used throughout the book as an "umbrella" of which Executive Coaching is considered a sub-set.

What business coaching is not

In the spirit of clarifying the boundaries and providing a definition of business coaching, it may also be helpful to describe what it is not.

Here are some illustrative examples:

➡ Expert consulting services to help solve a complex business problem.
Consulting? – Look under "Yellow Pages" for "Business Consulting".

➡ Long term relationship where a more experienced/qualified leader or peer provides support and guidance on professional development.
Mentoring? – Check your company internet for "Mentoring Services", or use the relevant professional association to find a mentor.

➡ Dealing with deeply personal matters of a psycho-social nature surrounding personal well being.
Counselling? – Seek out help from a qualified "Counsellor",

"Psychologist" or "Psychotherapist" (and speak to your own medical practitioner first).

⇒ Navigating the complex and covert world of internal politics to look for often undefined career ladders.
Internal Politics? – Seek out an HR Adviser (they should have connections and an understanding of how succession planning and talent management really takes place in the organisation).

⇒ Looking for some help to improve a basic skill or competence that has been identified as a weakness in a performance review.
Training Need? – Check out your training manual or speak to someone in your HR organisation who can advise you on a technical training solution.

⇒ Having a pleasant couple of hours conversation once a month that makes you feel listened to and loved.
Support? – Phone a friend!

Coaching styles

Now that we are clear on what we mean by business coaching, we need to look at different business coaching styles.

Different styles will encourage or lead to improved personal performance, and in turn improve bottom line business performance. To understand this, it is worthwhile looking at a spectrum of styles and the best fit for business coaching.

Within this context, it is useful to explore the distinction between "**directive**" and "**facilitative**" coaching. (Ref: Britner – Guest and Willis, 2004)

The "**facilitative coach**" views him/herself as having an equal stake in diagnosing the issues and identifying interventions to help improve performance. The person being coached sets the agenda with the coach providing a reality check and focussing on the pre-arranged goals throughout the coaching conversation. Feedback tends to be supportive rather than challenging and the overall coaching process is flexible rather than prescribed and rigid.

When to use a facilitative coaching style – example
An experienced senior manager is dealing with a significant change programme and needs support and coaching through an emerging and dynamic process.

The "**directive coach**" tends to focus on knowledge transfer. Often the coach will have a greater knowledge about a given area for improvement than the person being coached. A directive coach also focuses on creating tough individual challenges and assumes that results are mainly a matter of an individual's intentions, choices and actions.

When to use a directive coaching style – example
Someone who is new into a role and is short on time and experience to get to grips with some of the basic requirements required to start performing the role and make a difference.

Both styles can be appropriate for business coaching and they represent a spectrum rather than discrete entities. However, it is worthwhile making the distinction so that a prospective client can choose the style along the spectrum that best meets their business improvement needs. In the final analysis, establishing a successful coaching partnership comes down to personal chemistry and what works for a particular individual in a particular set of circumstances may not work for someone else.

As well as the distinction between "facilitative" v "directive" styles, it is worth considering whether you need coaching with an "individual" or "organisational" focus.

A focus at the "individual level" will look at the skills, experiences, successes and failures and track record of the person to date. It will also look wider to external factors (home and work influences) and some basic personality traits that underpin the behaviours exhibited in their role. Psychometrics, 360 degree feedback, performance appraisal data, peer feedback or a combination of all of these will usually be used to bring out the key performance issues to be addressed.

A focus at the "organisational level" will focus more on the specific task or project that the person is involved in and what they can learn from similar task or projects. Peer feedback and traditional appraisal data will be important. The views of the immediate supervisor and the individual's relationship to the supervisor play a key role, as do the longer term strategic objectives or goals of the organisation.

If we consider all these dimensions of coaching together (directive v facilitative and individual v organisational) then the differences can be summarised in Figure 4.

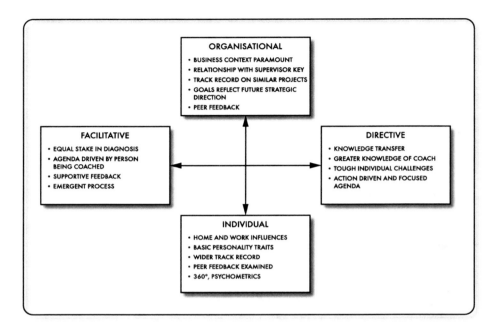

Figure 4. *Different dimensions of business coaching*

In reality the most effective business coaches will use a mixture of these styles and will be flexible enough to adapt to the changing needs of the client as the relationship evolves and the business context changes.

To help to understand where focused business coaching will make an improvement to business performance, a comparison of business coaching alongside other forms of coaching might be helpful. This is illustrated in Figure 5.

Understanding which coaching style best meets a specific need is an important part of ensuring best value is achieved from an investment in business coaching. This is considered further in Chapter 4 – "Getting the Best Value from Coaching".

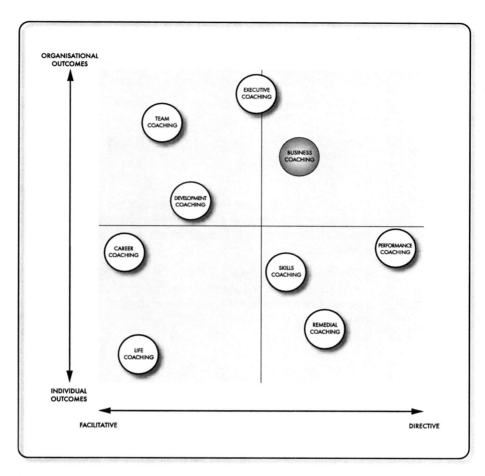

Figure 5. *Comparison of business coaching vs. other coaching types*

N.B. The definitions for Coaching Terms used in the diagram are taken from the CIPD definitions provided in their *Coaching and Buying Services Guide* (2005). These definitions are given in full in the Tools and Resources section at the end of this book.

CHAPTER SUMMARY

✓   To buy coaching effectively you need a clear definition and to understand where it fits into the organisation.

✓   Coaching continues to grow across all sectors of both private and business life.

✓   There are many and varied definitions of coaching available.

✓   Distinguishing business coaching from other interventions (e.g. mentoring) matters.

✓   Business Coaching can be defined as a series of regular conversations where the coach works in the best interests of the client towards goals that achieve improved business performance.

✓   Different coaching styles (facilitative vs. directive and individual vs. organisational) should be employed depending on the business outcome being pursued and the coach and client's preferences.

Chapter 3 – Sourcing the service for you

This chapter aims to help you make good decisions around sourcing a coach that will actually be right for a specific set of needs. It looks at:

➡ Assessing the coaching need

➡ When to use your own people

➡ Preparing a brief

➡ Finding the right coach

➡ Selection/matching process

➡ When to break the rules

Assessing the coaching need

– It is a service not a status symbol

Why would you approach buying the services of a coach any differently from buying any other business requisite? A high quality business coach costs many times more than an executive desk or new laptop and yet it is likely that the average executive will take more time and trouble researching and looking through specifications for the latter than for the coach.

The rules that govern any sound procurement investment are therefore a good starting point when considering how best to obtain a coach who matches both the needs of the individual and the business context they are working within. The first question to ask therefore is "Do I need a coach in the first place? (No different to "Do I really need to buy a new laptop when I am only using 10% of the functionality of the one I already have?)

Reasons for requiring a coach in the first place and some possible alternatives have already been considered in Chapter 1. To supplement this, and save time in making a decision on whether or not to buy in coaching, a simple checklist may help avoid a costly error.

A checklist is given below. If you have engaged a coach before, you can use this as a worked example.

Individual coaching need checklist:

➡ You have identified through a development plan a specific skill or behaviour you need for improved performance. ☐

➡ You have recently accepted a new role in an unfamiliar context, such as leading a major change initiative or significant business turnaround. ☐

➡ You have been identified for an executive position and you need to broaden your capacity and experience to take on such a role. ☐

➡ You tend to be task orientated and need to be more aware of the contribution of interpersonal skills and develop these. ☐

➡ You are from a strong technical background and need to become more capable in the areas of influencing others, understanding organisational issues and articulating non technical ideas. ☐

➡ You need to improve your team building skills. ☐

➡ You are faced with a significant increase in the scope of your responsibilities and are not sure how to handle this. ☐

➡ You have been asked to develop and articulate a new vision for your organisation. ☐

➡ You want to move from a more traditional leadership style to one that is less dominant and more open. ☐

➡ You need a confidential sounding board to help you work out how to turn strategies into action. ☐

If you have ticked one or more of the above boxes then consider hiring a coach.

When to use your own people

Let us assume that you have decided a coach will help you. The next question will be "Do I have to go externally and buy one in or is there someone in the organisation who can help me?" Although this book is aimed more at obtaining value from the use of external coaches it is worth briefly considering the internal coach as an option.

Often the organisation itself will determine whether this is in fact an option at all. Many smaller organisations will just not have internal coaching capability and have no economy of scale reasons for creating this capacity. However more and more large organisations, where coaching has become increasingly in demand, have created their own internal resource.

Case study

Prudential in the UK were early leaders in this area. Since 2003 they have been building an internal coaching capacity including establishing a "corporate university", allowing alumni to become "certified professional co-active coaches".

By 2005 Prudential had a pool of 200 internal accredited coaches at middle to senior management level and more than 400 more junior managers. (*People Management Magazine*, 1 Sept. 2005, pg. 46)

One of the main reasons for building internal capability is to allow a wider roll out of coaching across an organisation at a manageable cost (sometimes known as "scalability"). Many organisations have experience of using external coaches for supporting senior management development. However as organisations begin to realise the wider value of coaching, they look for ways to deliver it to a broader range of employees in a more cost effective way.

Another way to achieve coaching on a larger scale is to introduce the concept of "peer coaching". The benefits of peer coaching are clear in that the coach has internal knowledge of the organisation and the business context and provide a cost effective way of providing the support. (There is always the case to be made regarding the lost opportunity cost of distracting a senior manager away from their core role to do the coaching. However this is usually dismissed due to the double benefit learning that comes from both parties gaining from the relationship.)

John H. Zenger and Kathleen Stinnett, July 2006, pointed out in an article on Leadership Coaching that from their experience:

"Peer coaching implementations show that extremely beneficial results can be obtained. It works most effectively when those doing the coaching receive training on how to become effective coaches. But experience also shows that people with relatively short bursts of training prior to peer coaching can often provide great value to their peer partner. They become good sounding-boards regarding important issues. They provide a positive vehicle for testing out alternative courses of action, and once a path has been determined, they

can be a strong force for helping the client follow through on important commitments".

So it might well be an organisational driver which decides on whether the coach is sourced internally or externally but there are some underpinning reasons why one may be preferred to another. In the CIPD guide to *Coaching and Buying Coaching Services*, 2004, Jessica Jarvis provides a useful comparison on the use of internal and external coaches:

External coaches are preferable:

➡ For providing sensitive feedback to senior business leaders. For political reasons, this can be difficult for an internal coach

➡ For bringing specialist expertise from a wide variety of organisational and industry situations

➡ When individuals are concerned about "conflict of interests" and whether confidentiality will be observed

➡ For providing a wider range of ideas and experience

➡ For being less likely to judge and being perceived as more objective

➡ For asking questions that create a mindset change as their very lack of knowledge of the organisation can free them up to be more challenging

Internal coaches are preferable:

➡ When knowing the company culture, history and politics is critical

➡ When easy availability is desired

➡ For being able to build up a high level of personal trust over a period of time

➡ For not being seen to be "selling" consulting time

➡ For keeping costs under control (as the internal coaching could be free or less expensive than an external one)

Preparing a brief

So for the purposes of this chapter we will assume that a coach is required and that the preference is for an external one. The principles of good procurement practice are applicable and the most important thing to get right from the outset is a clearly defined list of requirements. Individual requirements will vary enormously, however there are some basic ground rules that should always be the starting point for defining the boundaries of the coaching contract.

Ground rules for specifying the coaching requirement:

➡ The coaching needs to be part of an overall development plan

➡ The plan will have been discussed and agreed with the business sponsor of the coaching (usually but not always the line manager)

➡ There should be clear boundaries including an agreed time frame and budget

➡ There must be tangible outcomes that can be reviewed throughout and at the end of the coaching contract

➡ The tangible outcomes must deliver improved business performance as well as individual performance

Finding the right coach

Once the individual needs are quantified then it is time to start looking for the type of coach or coaches who can deliver the required outcomes. The issue is where to start and how to evaluate whether the coach or coaches you choose are qualified to undertake the task.

 Fact

➡ The International Coaching Federation (ICF) has over 12,000 members in 80 countries

➡ The Association of Coaching (AC) in the UK is well established and has over 200 members on their books

➡ These are only two of an expanding number of bodies that have set themselves to improve standards and regulate the market in coaching. Others include the European Mentoring and Coaching Council (EMCC), the Coaching Psychology Forum (CPF) and the Chartered Institute of Personnel and Development (CIPD)

In addition to registered coaches working independently or with coaching companies there are also thousands of individuals who have set themselves up in varying coaching guises. In terms of formal coaching qualifications the market remains fairly unregulated with the number of accredited coaches being by far in the minority. However as we write, the desire to set some clear standards on accreditation combined with good practice in coaching supervision is growing almost as fast as the coaching market itself. Over the next few years the CIPD, ICF, EMCC and AC will continue to raise the bar on standards and create a much needed barrier to entry based on clearer accreditation rules for becoming a registered coach. Meanwhile accreditation could mean anything from a Master Certified Coach (MCC) with the ICF, which takes:

➠ 200 hours of coach specific training

➠ 2500 hours of coaching experience with clients

➠ Satisfactory completion of written and oral exams

➠ Demonstrated leadership within the profession

➠ Agreement to adhere to the Code of Ethics as outlined by the ICF

➠ Continued professional development to renew credentials every three years

compare this to:

➠ a few hours training over a weekend with a self-styled coaching organisation with a framed certificate to hang on your wall at the end . . .

Most coaches will lie somewhere in the middle of these two extremes.

So when considering hiring a coach, be diligent in asking the coach if they have been specifically trained in coaching skills and currently hold, or are in the process of acquiring, a recognised qualification from a reputable body. (See Tools and Resources for some examples of coaching qualifications).

Don't be misled into thinking a coach must be competent because they have either an impressive CV or set high fees. Referrals and testimonials from previous clients are useful, as are personal recommendations from people you trust. Also, ask the coach to describe the purpose of their coaching to you. As in all purchases remember the law of *caveat emptor* – buyer beware!

Using a rigorous approach

Accreditation is only one indication that a coach may be competent and there are other important factors that need to be taken into account when making a selection. These factors are again closely tied in to those that would be used in any professional procurement arrangement and as such a Request For Information (RFI) process or adapted version of one is a very good place to start. An example RFI letter and questionnaire is included in the Tools and Resources section at the end of this book.

An RFI can be applied at quite a simple level in a small organisation or at the other end of the spectrum can be undertaken as a large scale business intervention involving the HR Departments in partnership with Procurement and their business colleagues. A large scale case study is illustrated below.

Case study – large scale coaching review, BP

BP like many large organisations participated in the Coaching boom. In 2003 in the UK alone there was a fragmented external supply with more than 90 different organisations supplying more than 200 coaches.

50% offered purely coaching but the other 50% offered it as part of general consulting services.

There were a few large scale consultancies involved but the majority were individual sole traders from a variety of backgrounds. Daily rates varied from a few hundred pounds to over £5000 and rates seemed to increase when it was known that BP was the client, and within BP when the client business was associated with the more profitable Trading division.

Additional expenses varied from none at all to charging for travelling time and even phone calls to set up meetings. Travel expenses in one case included 1st Class Transatlantic flights. Coaching styles were undefined by either the coach or the client. Coaching was taking place at all levels in the organisations and neither the overall costs nor outputs were measured.

A coaching review process run by the Learning & Organisational Development function in conjunction with Procurement used a sophisticated RFI and selection process using professional HR and business managers to vet the supply chain across key success indicators. The result was a clearly articulated coaching requirement, a reduction in the supply base from 200 down to 60, a league table of preferred suppliers with competition introduced for the first time, recommended pricing levels for different types of coaching and an overall improvement in the control and supply with increased value at lower cost.

What should be included in an RFI process depends on the specific needs of both the individual and the organisation. Some of the key questions that should be considered would include:

- What is the track record of the individual/consultancy?
- Are there references available and can they be contacted?
- Do they have the resources to cope with the size of the project?

➡   What internal processes do they have to manage their own staff?

➡   How do they provide assurance for the client on confidentiality?

➡   What do they cost?

➡   How do they charge?

➡   Are they themselves professionally supervised and do they provide supervision arrangements for coaches under their control?

➡   What are their relevant qualifications and most recent training?

➡   Do they hold professional indemnity assurance?

N.B. A full checklist is given in the Tools and Resources section.

Using the HR department
In many, but not all, cases, coaches tend to go through the HR or L&OD Department of an organisation as the way of being "short listed" as available for coaching. Even if not the direct source, a good HR Department should nevertheless be well connected to their business clients and in turn be aware of the effective coaches being used in the organisation. The HR department may or may not be sophisticated enough to have a methodology for ranking or providing preferred supplier lists but it is likely that they will have some core data.

If you are a line manager, employee or business leader reading this and looking for a coach, then surprise your HR Department by giving them a clear definition of your needs, along with a request for someone who meets your RFI definition.

If you are an HR manager reading this, then impress your line manager, employee or business leader by supplying names of potential coaches clearly outlining their underpinning capabilities based on an RFI technique.

If you are a coach reading this, be prepared to complete this specification document when you receive it. Procuring coaching services via an RFI is the way the world is moving, so wow the client by having the data ready to hand and show you have your act together.

Selection/matching process

In larger organisations there may be a need to put in place a fairly sophisticated matching process where large numbers of coaches are required. This matching process is well worth understanding as the principles are applicable for any number of clients. A simple matching process is illustrated in Figure 6.

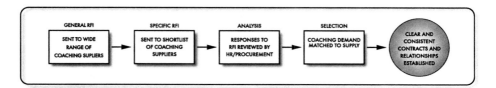

Figure 6. *A simple coach selection process*

Whatever you do, make sure that you have some way of vetting and that you end up with a reputable supplier. Individual coaches can be very charismatic, influential and powerful and can truly make a difference. Just make sure it is the difference that you intended! The basic underpinning requirement here is that the individual/organisation defines, owns and controls the coaching relationship and not the coach. There are some horror stories of this not being the case and in particular the examples of open ended contracts where the organisation basically becomes the "ATM" for the unscrupulous coach.

True story! – uncontrolled coaching

In an organisation that will remain nameless, the coach phoned the client and suggested they met for dinner. The client agreed and enjoyed a three hour dinner at an exclusive London restaurant selected by the coach that included expensive wine, malt whisky and cigars and a helpful but unstructured conversation on a coaching theme. One week later the client received an invoice for this to cover the coaching (rounded to half a day to include travel) together with the bill for dinner and a taxi fare home under expenses . . .

Is there some personal chemistry?

In emphasising the need for control and suggesting good practice in sourcing coaches using an adapted procurement method, it is also important to remember that ultimately coaching is about creating a good working relationship between two human beings. No matter how stringent you might be in specifying and selecting a coach, there is a big part of successful coaching that comes down to personal chemistry.

You need to select a coach that you connect with. So even after being provided with some names, you should shop around and meet with some coaches before finally selecting the one you would like to work with.

People often choose to work with people who are similar to them, which has advantages and disadvantages. Advantages include a feeling of trust and support and a rapid building of rapport. Disadvantages include the risk that sharing perspectives with your coach may mean you also share blind spots and miss opportunities for challenge, learning and improvement.

There are sophisticated ways of analysing what type of coaching style might match a particular individual. One way would be to use a "Learning Style Inventory". These are usually based on the work of David Kolb (1975). Using the Learning Style Inventory the individual can establish how they and their coach learn differently and therefore can be open to their challenge. For those interested in exploring the whole wider field of learning diagnostics then the most comprehensive and current example of this work is *The Learning Series* written by Dr. Peter Honey who has developed a suite of self-assessment online questionnaires dedicated to helping people become better all-round learners. Further information on *The Learning Series* and how to access it is contained in the Tools and Resources section.

In a practical sense, personal chemistry will often be a function of the importance you give to certain characteristics, and how you feel the coach displays them. When first meeting a coach some helpful pointers to explore might be:

PRESENCE: Interpersonal skills

➡ Are they easy to communicate with?

➡ Do they provide a "safe place" to have a conversation in?

➡ Do they put you at ease and quickly establish a good rapport?

MATURITY: Ability to be credible and authentic as a person

➡ Are they confident in themselves?

➡ Do you feel that they have experiences to share?

➡ Do they say when they don't know what the options might be?

FLEXIBILITY: Strong ethical sense and ability to adjust

➡ Can they "go with the flow" and work with ambiguity?

➡ Are there clear boundaries set from the beginning and reminders throughout?

➡ Are they challenging when they need to be and appreciative when it helps?

HONESTY: Solid knowledge of learning theories and change processes

➡ Do you feel that there is some structure to the conversations?

➡ Can they explain a model that they are working to?

➡ Do they offer examples and advice from a range of different sources?

POSITIVE FOCUS: Ability to plan, implement and manage a relationship

➡ Do they follow a plan they laid out at the outset?

➡ Do they generate a supportive and positive conversation?

➡ Is there a sense of progress?

It is good for all parties concerned that coaching is becoming more controlled and better regulated and that good practice in coaching supply is being developed with time. However we must make sure that this in turn does not throw out often intangible benefits that brought coaching into the business world in the first place.

 "I'd encourage professionalism, but it creates a dilemma, because there is still a magic to coaching – a unique specialness in one-to-one relationships that we don't want to drive out". Mike Conway, VP Resourcing and Development at Royal Dutch Shell, for a CIPD article in 2005.

Speaking to Mike in 2007, he said *"Two years on, my sentiments are the same and stronger. Also I would add today that as well as personal chemistry, it is very important that coaches have an appreciation of the business context in which they operate. This is not something usually picked up through formal coaching selection processes and maybe it should be".*

When to break the rules

Some of the best coaches may in fact be "one man bands" who don't meet all the difficult procurement criteria. They often come highly recommended by other people. In these circumstances it may be appropriate to consider them against other options, but make sure there are some references available from trusted sources with clear evidence of results being delivered.

A "try before you buy" approach is a good way forward and always remember that you have the right to say "no" to a coach at any time in the relationship.

CHAPTER SUMMARY

✓ Coaching should be given the same diligence as purchasing any important goods or services.

✓ Get clear on when to use internal versus external coaching.

✓ Apply some basic procurement practice –

- Specify individual requirements from the outset and stick to them

- Consider a range of possible suppliers

- Reduce the risks of untested suppliers by taking up references

✓ Matching processes can be basic or more sophisticated, but follow certain principles.

✓ Ultimately, personal chemistry will make or break the coaching relationship.

Chapter 4 – Getting the best value from coaching

In this chapter we will discover why coaching should probably cost less than you currently pay. We will investigate:

➡ How rates differ, depending on the coach's company status, e.g. Sole traders, associates to firms, employees of firms, etc.

➡ The pros and cons of going direct to individuals compared with using a larger supplier

➡ Case studies where buyers have found smart ways to avoid paying too much

Calculating the return on investment

As with all other investments in a business, it is good practice to calculate the rate of return you expect and subsequently receive from a coaching programme. This is notoriously difficult as there are so many other factors affecting an individual's performance. Nevertheless, an estimate can be very useful when assessing the effectiveness of a programme when comparing it to other people is development activity. Evaluating your coaching programme is covered in depth in Chapter 6.

Case study

More and more studies point to positive results. For example, a 2001 Manchester Review study of 100 executives documented the ROI for executive coaching at 5.7 times the initial investment.

A more recent Zenger Folkman study looked at the impact of managers and leaders who increased their effectiveness as coaches. This research shows that managers who are highly effective at coaching their direct reports have significant impact on the performance of their organisations.

We will look at both the costs and benefits in this chapter. The benefits side of the equation can be split into outputs and enablers:

Quantifiable benefits of coaching – example outputs

➡ Increased sales performance £

➡ Improved cost performance £

➡ Reduction in project delays vs. estimate £

➡ Reduction in staff turnover (saving in recruitment and training costs) £

➡ Reduction in levels of sickness absence £

➡ Increase in value to the business of the individual (sometimes known as human capital) £

Less quantifiable benefits – example enablers

➡ More harmonious working relationships within a team

➡ Healthier stress levels

➡ Better quality services provided internally or externally by the individual

➡ Smarter decision making

➡ A positive change in the culture within a department

➡ Ability to demonstrate a wider range of leadership styles

When to measure the benefits

Some of the benefits of coaching have a lag time attached, making return on investment calculations more complex. For example, developing a manager's leadership abilities will not result in immediate sales performance improvements.

To help with decision making about future programmes, the costs and benefits should be compared at the end of the planned coaching programme. For a longer programme, interim reviews should be completed every six months.

Some managers take the view that "you don't fatten the pig by weighing it", and prefer to avoid in depth analysis of the effectiveness of a programme, until at least three months after the programme has been completed. They feel that continual measurement is only a distraction from the coaching process. Another advantage of this approach is that leaving the assessment until later, though this is not always practical, can take into account some of the lag effect of benefits.

Why most buyers of coaching pay too much

There are some tell tale signs that are usually present where a buyer is paying too much or not getting enough value. These include:

➡ The organisation failing to clearly define what they want and need

➡ The client failing to clearly define what they want and need

➡ No mechanism to ensure that the coach's time is being used efficiently and/or effectively

➡ No process to evaluate the effectiveness of the investment

➡ No mechanism to stop the coaching relationship from losing focus

➡ Clients are staying with the same coaches beyond the original period agreed, without any scrutiny

➡ A lack of objectivity in the selection and evaluation process

➡ A lack of commitment to the process from the client

➡ A lack of market knowledge by the buyer leading to higher than necessary rates

How much is too much?

The bills from the coaching provider are only part of the equation. To borrow a term used in procurement departments, it is useful to consider the Total Cost of Ownership (TCO). As discussed in Chapter 3, buyers need to take at least as much care over procuring coaching services as they would over procuring laptops and other capital equipment, with the added complexity of personal chemistry being an important criteria in selection. The concept of TCO can be used when comparing coaching to other management development activities.

There are several elements to the costs of buying coaching:

The bill for coaching

INVOICE

Description: Executive Coaching Programme for Management Team of 10. Six-month programme, monthly sessions for each individual. Coach to observe two management meetings.

Fee from the coach for the total programme	£22,000
Third party costs e.g. psychometric testing @£500 per person	£5,000
Management fees from the HR Consultancy supplying coaches	£13,000
Travel and accommodation and telephone expenses	£6,000
Opportunity cost of man hours spent by the usually highly paid client	£10,500
Total bill	**£56,500**

We will look at each of these items individually:

1. Coach fees

There is huge variation in the rates charged for coaching. These are usually quoted in terms of daily rates and start at as little as £250 for new small or medium enterprise coaches, rising to £1200 – £1500 for a trained and experienced corporate business coach to well over £5,000 for a top CEO coach. These vary around the UK, with a higher rate typically in London and the South East.

 "A six month arrangement with a highly qualified, highly experienced coach can run between $15,000 and $30,000." Source: a recent article from the Harvard Business Review, by Lauren Keller Johnson 2007.

They also vary according to the industry sector the client is in. For example, the voluntary sector and traditionally lower margin businesses such as retail, experience lower rates than the "more affluent" sectors such as Financial Services and Oil and Gas. Even within one organisation, some divisions are prepared to pay significantly different rates to others. For example, the Exploration division in the oil industry will typically pay significantly higher fees than their Retail division, as the pressures on cost control are lower.

The Chartered Institute for Personnel Development (CIPD) publish market rates for coaching for its members, though the health warning is to be wary of regional and sector variations.

An alternative model is the **retainer fee**, typical in the marketing or PR sectors, where the coach can be called on at any time, usually up to a certain financial or time limit. This typically includes one meeting or call per month plus ad hoc email and telephone contact. This can be particularly useful for a change management situation, where the client may need support at shorter notice and on an ad hoc basis.

The difference between two suppliers' quotes may be a result of one including travel costs or psychometric testing, which the other lists as extras. It is useful for the buyer to ask for any other costs that a coach would expect to invoice to check it's all covered by the hourly or daily rate in the RFI.

2. Third party costs

Where an extra service is proposed, such as psychometric testing and feedback, this will incur a mark-up from the firm you have contracted with. It is worth checking that you don't already have this resource within your organisation, or it can be accessed at a lower rate from another supplier. If not, remember that the level of mark-up can be negotiated.

Fees	Pros	Cons
Hourly or daily rate	Pay for what you use Transparent Easily monitored Easily compared to other providers	Last minute cancellations may still be charged (subject to the terms and conditions agreed) More susceptible to creeping upward charges
Retainer	More predictable costs for the business where the limits are adhered to Easier to get budget approval Available for short notice and immediate response	May not use the services to the value paid – just like a gym membership Can rack up costs if the contract is not strictly defined and the client goes over the retainer limit

Each coaching provider is likely to have their own preferred method of profiling such as Myers Briggs, OPQ, DISC, Insights, etc. It is worth checking that the psychometric being suggested by the coach is indeed the best value option. Many organisations will have access to their own profiling tools at a lower rate, or on a licence that is already paid for. Always check with your HR department to see what tools are already available.

3. Management fees
Depending on your contract arrangements, these may be noted separately or bundled in with the coach fees. Where they are bundled in, they will form between 25% and 75% of the daily rate fees. They cover the cost of sales and marketing, account management, billing and credit control, reporting, professional indemnity insurance, training and development and of course, profit margin.

 One tip to save costs is where you are using a large volume of coaching time, it can be advisable to strip the management fee out of the daily rate and negotiate this separately.

4. Travel and accommodation expenses
These should be passed on at cost with no mark-up, and the coach should follow the same travel policy as their clients. Where you have special deals with hotels or airlines, it is often more cost effective to book and pay for these items directly.

5. Cost of man hours spent by the client

This is an area of cost most often overlooked as it is hidden to the budget holder. The opportunity cost of the time spent by the client in coaching sessions should be significantly higher than the individual's loaded salary cost per hour. This is because the client could be spending that time in a more effective development activity. This could be with a more effective coach, or a training or mentoring programme.

One of the attractions of coaching is that it offers short, sharp, tailored interventions rather than days of generic training. Where the coaching is not producing an improved performance however, this cost can become significant.

Getting more value for your coaching investment

As most coaches will be charged on a daily rate basis, some administration effort to organise a full programme can improve their productivity by as much as 100%.

Case study – getting the same value for half the investment

At a major UK Telecommunications company, the top 50 managers were sent on a Leadership Development Programme and each assigned an executive coach for a six month period. The coach was charged out at £1,500 per day, and planned a half-day session with each client. If one client changed the appointment at short notice or was unavailable, and the coach only saw one client per day, they still charged the full-day rate. Typically, the clients only spent a maximum of 2 hours with the coach in a session.

By reviewing the actual pattern of sessions after the programme, the HR manager analysed the spend and activity. She modelled a different contract: Had the coach planned in three sessions per day and charged per session rather than per day, the bill would be cut in half. For the next coaching programme, she also shared the cost information with the clients and encouraged them to keep to appointments.

➡ Where the coach has several clients within an organisation, pre-arrange three or even four coaching sessions on the same day, well in advance.

➡ Arrange a mix of group and individual coaching in a day to address common development needs balanced by individual time and focus.

➡ Consider a mix of telephone and face-to-face sessions, to fit more contact time into the coach's day.

➡ Consider the geographical range of costs. The South East of England is much more expensive so agreeing London rates for locally based coaches around the UK is a guaranteed way to pay too much. As many highly qualified professionals have migrated out of the South East to the regions, there is a wealth of talent available at significantly lower rates.

➡ Demand value from your management fee. The mark up that you are paying on top of the coach's rate is negotiable and should be providing benefits to you, rather than just profit to the coaching firm. Ask for a regular account management meeting to review delivery against the contract, monthly reporting on progress, evidence of CPD from the coaches and organisational themes that are emerging from the coaches' experience.

➡ Consider the length of engagement and review progress regularly. What starts off as a three month contract subject to review can easily be extended indefinitely. It is in the coach's financial interests to extend the arrangement. It may be the right decision but there is clearly room for a biased judgement to be made.

➡ Use your coaches to help you prioritise investment in other management development areas. Your coaches are ideally placed to spot the areas of most need experienced by their clients, and are usually well versed in the types of management development activities that are available. See Chapter 7 for more on this topic.

Some pricing models

As already shown in this chapter, the way fees are presented to clients varies enormously. In summary, here are some of the typical ways to determine the contract rate used by individual coaches and coaching firms:

➡ Hourly rate vs. session rate vs daily rate

➡ Target number of clients in a day

➡ Face-to-face vs. telephone coaching

➡ Fixed term or open ended

➡ Retainer

➡ Payment on results

➡ Separate management fee

Case study – worked example: who gets better value?

Company A brings in coaches to work with five of their nine managers. The arrangements have been made directly between the managers and coaches. A retainer rate is agreed for one coach and a daily rate for another four coaches. The rates include the management fees of the separate coaching suppliers. The contract is open ended and no up front performance measures have been set.

Company B brings in a coach to work with their nine managers. The programme is fixed at six months with an evaluation process based on performance targets agreed after the first session with the MD of the nine managers. The coach is asked to provide feedback to the MD on team effectiveness and organisational structure issues, after sitting in on the management team meeting every three months. The company pays a per session rate for the coach.

One year on . . .
Company A is still paying the monthly retainer to one coach. One of the managers being coached has left the firm. The other three are still using their coaches, two can demonstrate improved results, the other manager cannot. The four managers without a coach are continuing to perform to a similar level to one year ago.

Company B has seen a big improvement in the team's performance. The MD has made some changes to the team structure after the six month programme finished. Five of the managers continue to work with the original coach, two are working with a different coach, focusing on financial management skills. The other two managers are attending professional development training instead of coaching.

How to negotiate the best deal

The model for using tried and tested procurement practices was outlined in Chapter 3. Assuming that you have some existing arrangements that may not have gone through a rigorous process, it may be advisable to conduct a review of existing arrangements:

1. Describe exactly what you need, why and for how long
2. Consider and price alternative solutions
3. Describe the tangible and intangible benefits you are looking for
4. Define the evaluation criteria for bids
5. Conduct an open procurement process (not just your old favourites)
6. Include the key stakeholders in the evaluation
7. Use procurement expertise in the contract negotiations
8. Use a master agreement or contract (including important terms and conditions such as the need for confidentiality and cancellation fees.)
9. Check credentials and references
10. Hold the winning supplier(s) to the contract

The role of the client

There are various stakeholders in the coaching relationship as shown in Figure 7. The client is the most significant player not only in the role of receiving coaching, but also in their often overlooked role of ensuring that the organisation gets value for money for the investment in their coaching.

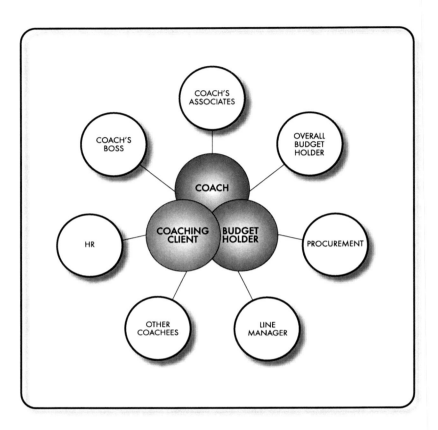

Figure 7 *Stakeholders in the coaching process*

For coaching to be highly cost-effective, using some of the themes already established in chapter 3, then the client should:

1. Clearly define his or her coaching goals, in the context of the organisation

2. Follow an objective coach selection process, supported where appropriate by the HR / Learning & Organisational Development department

3. Approach the experience with an open minded, learning mindset

4. Be aware of the costs and other options

An awareness of the total cost to the business of their coaching resource will assist the client in making more objective decisions on whether the contract should be terminated, extended or changed in scope.

One way to avoid wasting money on coaching is to check that the manager in question is ready and open to coaching. A simple questionnaire covering topics such as "do I have some idea of my coaching goals" and "do I have time – or can I make time – for coaching" can identify those individuals for whom coaching is not the most effective route to performance improvement. There is a short "Are You Ready For A Coach?" questionnaire that can cover this potential pitfall, in the Tools and Resources section.

There is an enormous body of evidence that suggests that the real benefits from any developmental experience come from what happens after the "event", whether it be a class, a seminar, an e-learning programme or a week-long residential programme. One of the reasons to invest in coaching is to capitalise on training activity and turn the new skills or knowledge into real business benefits rather than a happy memory. A regular coaching arrangement can keep the new information top of mind and ensure the client is focussed on what they are going to do differently, and how that new information is going to be applied.

CHAPTER SUMMARY

✓ Many organisations are paying too much for coaching compared to the value they receive.

✓ There are some simple ways to squeeze more value from your coaching investment:

- Encourage clients to be clear about their coaching needs, and to keep these updated

- Use a rigorous procurement process (outlined in Chapter 3)

- Consider the various pricing models on offer and design the one that suits your organisation

- Identify the Total Cost of Ownership of your coaching resources and communicate this to clients

- Identify the value that can be gained from coaching (such as ensuring sustained benefit from training courses and prioritising development investment) and feed this in to rest of the management development agenda

- Carry out regular reviews of the coaching arrangements to ensure they are still appropriate

Chapter 5 – Who should manage the coaching process

 "In my experience of working with many organisations, when the executives are left entirely alone to manage the coaching contracts themselves then dramatically different rates are paid for similar services, a weird and wonderful collection of different coaches of varying abilities show up and there is no clear idea or even interest in finding out if it is effective. It might be good for an unscrupulous coach showing up to make a quick buck but it does nothing for the credibility of serious coaches, coaching as a whole or indeed the practice of sound executive coaching." – Ian Hunter, Founding Partner of Orion Partners, and author of *The Seven Steps of Executive Coaching*.

We have already looked at a number of ways to get more value from coaching: defining exactly what type of coaching is needed, how it will fit with other development work that is going on and where to get it. We have covered negotiating the contract and setting the right objectives.

Imagine that the first session is booked for next week and you are thinking about how the process will be managed. What role, if any, should HR play? Should the client do it all themselves? Where does the line manager fit in?

In order to examine this in more detail, in this chapter we will look at:

- ➡ The key players and their respective agendas
- ➡ The owner of the budget
- ➡ The pros and cons of the coach being the budget holder
- ➡ The ideal scenario
- ➡ The pitfalls

Business coaching is a significant investment in terms of both time and money. Like any other investment it needs to be carefully managed as a business process to ensure that there is an acceptable return on that investment.

The key inputs are **time, money** and **skill. Business performance improvements** are the key outputs or outcomes. The components of performance improvement include the client's skill set, level of self awareness, capability as a manager and leader and their contribution as a team member.

Figure 8 shows how coaching can impact business performance. In managing the process, the indicators at each stage can be monitored to ensure that the coaching investment is having the desired effect.

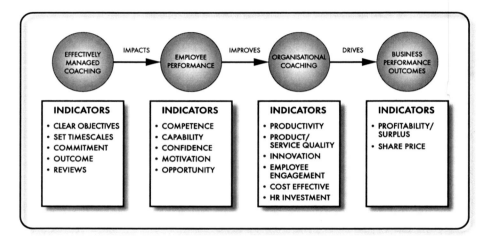

Figure 8. *The impact of effective business coaching*

The key players

We have already looked at the main roles in any coaching arrangement, and we will turn now to how these people can effectively manage the coaching contract. In addition to the key players, as shown in Figure 7, there are several other stakeholders.

Each of the key players has their own set of objectives but they must overlap to achieve a suitable outcome and benefit for the organisation. If any one player takes too much control over the process, there will be an unbalanced and possible detrimental outcome for the business.

To ensure that coaching is effective, the needs of each of the key stakeholders must be met. Their agendas may be different.

Client's agenda

In any coaching relationship, the client will be looking for personal development. In addition, they may:

➡   Want the status symbol of being associated with a highly paid/high profile coach

➡   Perhaps want a low key approach (in case the reason for seeking a coach is misunderstood)

➡   Want the coaching sessions to focus on personal as well as business topics

Budget holder's agenda

An important stakeholder. The budget holder may be the line manager, HR Manager or the client themselves. They will want to make sure that:

➡   The money (and time) is well spent

➡   There is evidence of a benefit from the coaching process

➡   The duration of the commitment is clear so that they can plan their budget

➡   There is reassurance that the coaching programme is the best match for the client's needs rather than the coach's needs

Coach's agenda

In any coaching relationship, the coach will be looking to:

➡   Create a helping and supportive relationship for the personal development of the client

➡   Have a receptive client to work with

➡   Extend the duration and breadth of contract where possible

➡   Identify opportunities to secure coaching or training work for their associates

➡   Use a particular set of preferred techniques or experiment with other techniques

As you can see from the key players agendas, there is just as likely to be a potential conflict, as there is an opportunity for a mutually beneficial arrangement.

In order to satisfy the distinct requirements of each key player, a robust framework for selecting, matching, managing and evaluating the coaching process should be used.

If HR are not the budget holders, they still have a useful role to play in determining the coaching strategy, policing the management framework around the use of coaching and identifying and sharing the learning from the coaching activity across the organisation.

The other interested parties may have something to offer the process, or may have the power to derail the matching process. Examples include:

➡ The line manager insisting on a particular focus for the coaching programme

➡ Other clients promoting the techniques that their coach is using

➡ The coach's boss wanting to match a particular coach for logistical reasons

➡ The overall budget holder wanting to reduce the cost of the programme

➡ The coach's associates are wanting to try out a particular profiling technique

➡ The HR department want to insist on coaches accredited by a particular coaching body

➡ Procurement are keen to narrow down the approved supplier list

It is therefore worth checking the needs and possible contributions of each stakeholder.

Does it matter who owns the budget?

In some smaller firms, the client and the budget holder can be one and the same person. In other cases, the line manager or HR department may be holding the budget.

Where a separate department holds the budget, the client may not be aware of the value of the investment the organisation is making. This can lead to the coach's time being undervalued by the client and where the terms of the agreement are not visible there is a danger that money can be wasted. For example, the coach may charge for late cancellations.

Pros and cons of the client being the budget holder

There are a number of advantages to the client holding the budget:

➡ The client knows the costs and the terms of the agreement

➡ The client is likely to take more responsibility for getting significant benefits from the coaching sessions

➡ The client is able to compare the value of this activity with other possible solutions

There are also downsides:

➡ The client may not value themselves highly enough to justify the spend on coaching

➡ The client may over inflate the value of their development and pay too much

➡ The personal relationship with the coach may cloud the commercial judgement of the client and result in the contract being extended without justification

➡ There is less accountability for the client to show benefits to justify the investment

Ideal scenario

Given these advantages and disadvantages, the ideal situation is for the client to hold the budget, and to have support from HR and procurement professionals. Their line manager should agree on the expected outcome from the coaching programme.

1. The client has responsibility for the budget

The line manager agrees a sum of money for personal development for the individual and agrees the expected personal outcomes and business deliverables. This amount is based on the value of the employee to the organisation, and potential of the individual to develop. Many organisations use a simple "Potential/Performance Quadrant" to rank employees and prioritise development resources (Figure 9).

Based on this analysis, decisions on how to deal with each individual can be made. For example, move Fred to a more suitable role (either inside or outside the organisation), give coaching and stretching assignments to Ann, provide motivational coaching for Bill and Sarah and manage Alan and Jo's expectations that they are unlikely to be promoted.

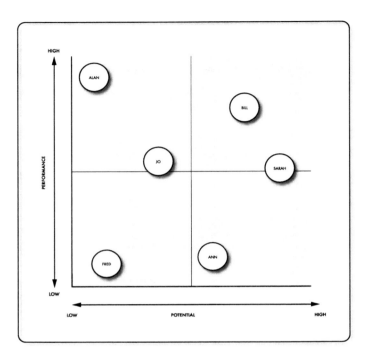

Figure 9 *Potential/performance quadrant*

The client decides where to spend the money, from a range of possible investments. The HR department may have made it easy to access and assess a range of development activities, which address the client's needs. In larger organisations, this is often published on the organisation's intranet site so that it can be updated centrally. There may be a preferred supplier list with negotiated rates available.

2. A consistent framework is used
HR professionals should be used as a resource to create the framework, which represents best practice in the use of coaching. This framework should include the following elements:

1. A definition the need for coaching as one tool in a range of development options

2. An identification the development objectives for the individual, and the type of coaching required

3. A process for matching the coach to the client

4. A process for managing the coaching activities

5.   A review and evaluation stage

6.   A tapping in to the coach's perspective on the business (see Chapter 7 The Future of Coaching)

7.   An influential champion ensures that this framework is used consistently, and maintained over time

3. Key performance indicators or performance objectives are used

As with other investments, a clear outcome should be set, and a timescale agreed to achieve it. The objectives to achieve the outcomes will be driven by the type of coaching need that is identified. Some examples are shown below:

Table 5.1. *Examples of objectives for coaching programmes*

Type of need	Example objective
Remedial	"No grievances are raised against this individual in the six months following the coaching programme"
Performance improvement	"This year's performance targets are exceeded"
Specific skill development	"Feedback from subsequent presentations demonstrates a significant improvement in presentation skills"
General skill development	"Feedback from colleagues and line manager demonstrates a significant improvement in skills"
Developing a strategic perspective	"A strategic rather than operational view is taken of the business. Examples of more strategic decision making are demonstrated"

Progress towards the desired outcomes can be reviewed at regular interviews and this helps to keep the coaching programme focused. It is very common to find that no sooner is the initial objective achieved than the client sets new, more stretching, goals.

The sceptical budget holder may see this as unnecessary selling of extra services by the coach, and a sense check with the client's line manager is helpful here to check that these new goals are relevant to the business context.

Pitfalls

Here are some signs that the coaching process is not being managed well:

For the organisation:

1.   String of bills for missed or cancelled appointments

2.   Sudden expansion of demand for coaching at the expense of all other management development activities

3.   Renewal or extension of coaching contracts without an evaluation process

4.   Several new coaches are working in the organisation without any procurement or matching process

For the client:

5.   Demand for coaching from high potential individuals is not met in favour of cheaper "one size fits all" courses

6.   Line managers wash their hands of all development and appraisal activities (line managers have asked the coach to prepare appraisals on the client – and the coach has agreed)

7.   High potential individuals are not supported in new roles or on new projects and are struggling to achieve targets

8.   Some clients are tolerating coaching sessions because they have been told it will be career limiting not to take part

CHAPTER SUMMARY

✓ The coaching process should be managed like any other business process, and its value compared to other possible solutions.

✓ There are many ways to manage the coaching process and their effectiveness varies.

✓ The agendas of the key players (Client, Coach and Budget Holder) must be balanced.

✓ The outcomes (changes in skill level, behaviour and performance) as well as the inputs (time, money and skills) should be specified.

✓ The objectives of the coaching investment should be defined in terms of value to the business as well as the individual.

✓ HR can provide a robust framework for line managers to use to ensure best value is achieved.

Chapter 6 – Evaluating coaching

It would be unreasonable to expect a money back guarantee from a coach, but not unreasonable to expect some measurable improvement against an agreed set of objectives. After all, the investment in time alone has probably been over six months – or more. The purpose of coaching in a business context is not to make the client feel better about themselves (although is almost always does!) The purpose is to change the way a client operates within an organisation to the benefit of that organisation and in ways that are observable to the individual and those around them. Easy to say, but harder to actually do and therein lies the issue of the evaluation of coaching.

So when do you know that coaching has made a difference and helped the client achieve the agreed objectives?

This chapter will:

➡ Define success for coaching evaluation

➡ Describe some evaluation methods

➡ Offer an ROI calculation

➡ Explore the intangible benefits

➡ Identify signs that value is being lost

➡ Suggest how to act on the results of evaluation

➡ Identify when to stop using coaching

Defining success for coaching evaluation

An effective evaluation tells the organisation whether or not coaching was a worthwhile investment.

Success at a very basic level could be that an organisation even bothers to undertake any evaluation. Most organisations will agree that it is important to do some evaluation, but it is often forgotten in the frantic pursuit of everyday business life. At best a large proportion of organisations rely on little more than anecdotal evidence to measure effectiveness.

The issue is about how to establish tangible benefits from anything which has its roots in human behaviour. Those trying to quantify the benefits of training have grappled with the same issue. Without an evaluation process, coaching will become of one of these interventions that becomes yet another leap of faith rather than anything measurable.

 "When you create a culture of coaching, the result may not be directly measurable in dollars. But we have yet to find a company that can't benefit from more candour, less denial, richer communication, conscious development of talent, and disciplined leaders, who show compassion for people." (Sherman and Alyssa Freas, *The Wild West of Executive Coaching*, *Harvard Business Review*, November 2004.)

Evaluation methods

The training analogy is a useful one and the model introduced many years ago by Donald Kirkpatrick (1994) for assessing training effectiveness is the industry standard. According to this model (illustrated below) evaluation should always begin at level 1, and then, as time and budget allows, should move sequentially through levels 2, 3 and 4. Information from each level serves as the base for the next level evaluation and therefore each successive level represents a more precise measure of the effectiveness along the chain.

Kirkpatrick's model is illustrated below:

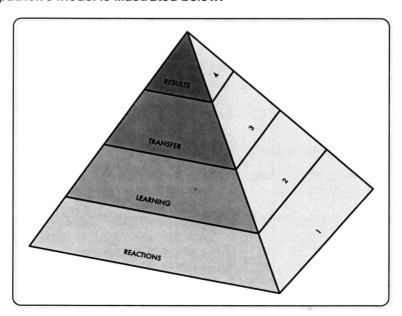

For coaching evaluation, most organisations are working at the very basic "reaction" level 1. This is usually a "Happy Sheet" or simple feedback form. The analogy of training and the Kirkpatrick model would suggest a more systematic evaluation of coaching through all the levels may help establish that changes have taken place at more than just level 1. Some suggested indicators for coaching are illustrated below, covering levels 1 and 2.

N.B. The Tools and Resources section includes a sample evaluation questionnaire.

Level 1 reactions

Individual/coach indicators:

➡ The coach was clear upfront at the contracting phase on boundaries and objectives

➡ The coach was trustworthy and delivered against agreed commitments

➡ Ad hoc support was available, and a good relationship established

➡ Appointments were kept, basic logistics were in place, written records were produced, and in general there was a professional approach to the coaching arrangements

➡ Overall, there was good personal chemistry and the coaching was felt to be helpful

Level 2 learning

Individual indicators:

➡ Developmental insights were gained from the coaching

➡ Tangible development needs for skill and knowledge gaps were identified

➡ A revised and more relevant personal development plan was put in place as a result of the coaching

➡ New career, promotion, transfer options came up and were explored as a natural outcome of the coaching conversation

However, for a real organisational benefit to be realised, we would recommend that there is increased focus for business coaching at around the levels 3 and 4 in the Kirkpatrick model. Levels 3 and 4 look at behavioural and business performance changes. For a real organisational benefit to have been realised, then this will show up under some of the indicators for levels 3 and 4, but particularly level 4. This logic is consistent with our earlier definitions of business coaching with the emphasis on improving business results. The "bottom line" for us is that the coaching benefit is in fact, the "bottom line"!

Case study

The work by David Gray (2005) in the EMCC. Journal (Principles and Processes of Coaching Evaluation) supports the idea that the benefits of coaching should be seen on the bottom line. He also believes that most organisations only evaluate at level 1, where he would emphasise that it is possible to evaluate from a wide range of perspectives as covering all four Kirkpatrick levels. In a summary of his recommendations Gray states that "evaluation of coaching should:

➡ Be done as a matter of course and be pre-planned, and the process agreed before the coaching takes place.

➡ Include ethical considerations including who should have access to evaluation data.

➡ Be undertaken on a collaborative basis by all relevant stakeholders, the coaches, clients and sponsors, so that all perspectives are acknowledged.

➡ Include goals or outcomes that are negotiated between the stakeholders, recognising these may change and be renegotiated during the coaching process.

➡ Ensure that as well as tangible outcomes, the focus includes interactive processes within the coaching relationship.

➡ Include a focus that goes beyond the coaching relationship to include the selection of coaches and the management of the matching process."

In applying the Kirkpatrick model to the coaching process some examples of types of measures that could be used to identify outcomes of coaching at Levels 3 and 4 are described below. The emphasis here is on coaching outcomes which should be observable and verifiable, not necessarily by an in-depth study, but at least by examining improvements against the agreed individual and organisational targets:

Level 3 transfer

Examples of behavioural indicators:

- Improved 360° feedback results
- Increased self-confidence
- Improved performance against annually set performance contracts
- Promotion to a more challenging role
- Higher profile on leadership events
- Entry into "HIPO" schemes (high potential)
- Being given more challenging responsibilities within the role

Level 4 results

Organisational Indicators:

- Enhanced interactions at the leadership team level
- Improved scores in people attitude surveys
- Improved business performance against business performance contracts
- Organisation is rated highly externally and benchmarks well

An ROI calculation for coaching

The ultimate in the evaluation of the coaching process in a business context would be a simple formula for calculating the return on investment. This has been described in a training context as "level 5" on an extended Kirkpatrick scale by Jack J Phillips (1986). Phillips would see that at "level 5", an ROI could be calculated by converting routine business measures such as productivity and quality improvement to monetary value (benefit) and comparing them to the coaching programme cost to yield an ROI value. This calculation is just as relevant to coaching, and with some planning upfront it should be relatively easy to capture some hard benefits for any particular coaching assignment.

There are many consultancies and products that offer measurement or evaluation tools. There's also a case to be made for using such external agencies as a more independent and objective source of a valuation than internally driven measurement. However, using an external source will always add to the cost and in itself reduce the ROI. Without using an external supplier, but applying a similar approach will often be the best option and a useful ROI formula for this is shown below:

Formula

Return On Investment (%) = $\dfrac{\text{Benefit (£)} - \text{cost of coaching} \times 100}{\text{cost of coaching}}$

(ROI)

Where "benefit" = productivity increase, quality improvement, increased sales, etc.

Using such a formula effectively is dependent upon a good estimate of the benefit in £s, which in turn drives the need for specific and quantifiable goals and outcomes. This approach helps create rigour in the coaching contract if these goals or outcomes are agreed upfront. It also creates a more concrete discussion by linking individual improvement to business improvement, usually by identifying individual performance contracts which track organisational targets. For example, on a manufacturing site, a senior executive could commit to a personal target of increasing the ROACE (Return On Average Capital Employed) by a specific value over a specific period.

A suggested ROI process for a coaching assignment is given below:

Process

1. Agree evaluation method and measures at the start of the coaching process

2. Ensure measurement mechanisms are in place

3. Collect data at the start and end of coaching assignment

4. Isolate the impact of coaching from other initiatives. E.g. what percentage of the improvement can be attributed to the coaching intervention?

5. Convert the data to monetary value. E.g. Reduction in staff attrition of 5% = £65,000

6. Tabulate and calculate the coaching costs. N.B. Include all fees and expenses

7. Calculate the ROI

   Return On Investment (%) = $\dfrac{\text{Benefit (£)} - \text{cost of coaching} \times 100}{\text{cost of coaching}}$

   (ROI)

8. Identify intangible benefits, e.g. better team atmosphere

9. Use conclusions to evaluate coaching versus other training providers or possible interventions

Case study

At the end of 2006, the MD of an electronics company called in a coach to discuss the development of his management team. After turning the firm around from the brink of a shut down, the team had reached a profitable position again. The US owners were now expecting the positive results not only to continue, but to grow significantly. The MD knew that his team needed to move their performance up a level, shifting their thinking from the operational day-to-day, towards a more strategic level, in order to reach the stretching new targets.

He asked the coach to work with each member of the team individually once a month. In addition, he asked her to sit in on the management meetings and suggest ways for the team to operate more effectively as a group.

The coaching sessions were different for each individual, based on their own starting point and management style. Some existing Belbin team roles analysis were supplemented by a more in depth psychometric analysis (Insights), which was also used as a team-building tool.

One year on, the team had indeed met their stretching target. Despite one of the team being on maternity leave for six months, the team had been strong enough to allow the MD to take up a part time role in another division of the firm.

Using the Return On Investment calculation, the firm had gained a growth in Operating Income of 9 times the coaching investment. The MD is convinced that coaching has made a major contribution to the firm's impressive results, *"I am committed to continuing with the coaching programme. I know how much I value the coaching sessions and I get consistently positive feedback from the management team. Even as the pressure on costs and budgets grows from the US, this will be the last thing to go."*

Updating the ROI concept – the balance scorecard approach

A good way to establish coaching in a credible way within an organisation is to use the appropriate and current business language used in other disciplines. This allows the translation of the coaching benefits into whatever business model that is currently operating in that organisation. Beyond a basic ROI calculation is the concept of a "Balanced Business Scorecard" which is now an accepted tool in a business context. A version of this tool has been adapted and shown to work extremely well for coaching in a real life business situation by Logica. A brief outline of their approach is given in the case study below:

Case study – Logica

Since 2001, Logica has been building a strong and successful internal coaching capability. Based on a competency framework defining leadership qualities for a newly merged top team, coaching was introduced as a key component of a Leadership Development Programme and 15 managers were included in the first programme. The result was powerful, with 5 of the 15 managers promoted to the Executive Committee and zero attrition rate during the Programme for the others. As part of developing an ROI methodology for this type of programme, Paul Barker, Director of Coaching at Logica from 2005, now Lead Partner at 121 partners, introduced the idea of using a Balanced Business Scorecard. It was chosen because it was:

➡ well established and respected by business leaders

➡ relatively simple

➡ helpful to convert nebulous words like "strategy" and "coaching" into broad but measurable goal sets

➡ rooted in business reality rather than psychological analysis

Using this approach, Alice Hurley, Internal Coach and Client Director, applied it to a business project she was involved with. The project related to helping a newly established team exploit an international marketing opportunity in the area of electronic passports, (shorthanded to the "e-identity project"). It was a challenge, as historically the company like many others found it hard to establish and utilise virtual teams across traditional and organisational boundaries, particularly in this case where there was a diverse range of skills to be utilised from technical through to marketing and sales. A team coaching approach was adopted very successfully and they developed and delivered:

➡ shared and SMART objectives

➡ team member profiles of strengths and weaknesses using the BELBIN tool

➡ a bespoke 360 feedback tool

➡ one-to-one coaching support to each team member

➡ 3 team workshops

The balanced business scorecard was introduced (a version of which has been reproduced below) and through using it Logica were able to record and demonstrate the bottom line business benefits delivered from this highly effective and impactful team coaching intervention.

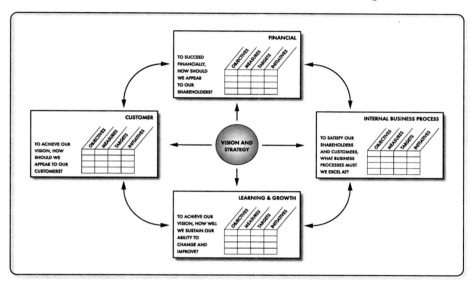

Figure 10. *Outline of Logica template for business balanced scorecard*

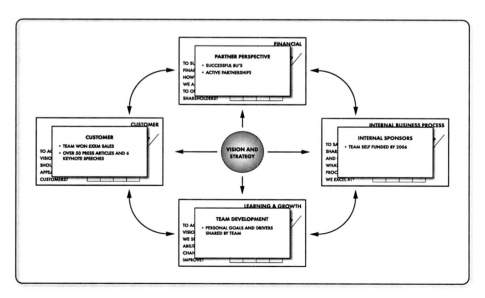

Figure 11. *Summary of balance scorecard targets for Logica Team coaching project*

Intangible benefits

There is of course more to coaching than just something that can be reduced to a set of numbers on a balance sheet. It is after all, a process that basically involves the interaction through conversation between two human beings. The softer benefits can include improvements like a more supportive and positive working atmosphere.

Story

David Nicholson, (previously an L&OD Director with BP in Asia-Pacific who now runs his own successful consultancy in Australia) would philosophically and consistently say: ". . . in a world where everyone focuses on trying to reduce everything to a set of numbers, businesses are never happy unless they can slap a KPI on it. Life isn't that simple, and they miss a trick. It is something about simply valuing the importance of human relationships in delivering something special without having to measure it. Taking time to understand people's underlying assumptions, espoused beliefs and values are what provide access to personal and organisational performance. Be wary about getting a KPI on this sucker, you cannot measure everything!"

Coach self assessment

It is advisable to ask the coach to complete the same evaluation process as the clients. The results can then be used to compare results for different clients as well as identifying any major disparities with the client's results.

Signs that you are not getting good value

In Chapter 4, we suggested some basic procurement practices to help make sure that you get good value from your coaching programme. When evaluating coaching in a systematic way, and using the various levels of the evaluation, 1 through to 4, throughout the coaching assignment (not just at the end) problems can be highlighted quickly. These problems include:

Pitfalls

"Creeping commitment" – The coaching programme is going beyond the original end date without scrutiny or sign off. This is a result of not agreeing clear milestones in delivery or product and a clear end point to the work. i.e. a recognisable deliverable.

"Additional costs" – These could arise from expenses over and above the day rate, such as five-star accommodation, frequent travel or business class travel. Where a retainer arrangement has been made, and the client has used more time than agreed, the extra costs can quickly add up.

"Multi-clienting" – Where a coach may be working with several clients in parallel for the same organisation. If they are not organising them effectively, this can compromise delivery of the programme within the desired timescales.

"Unplanned Days" – Numerous ad hoc days are added into the contract and intervening periods. This is a result of not agreeing a maximum number of sessions and fixed costs from the outset.

Breakdown in Communication – The person who selects the supplier, tenders and negotiates the contract may be someone different to the person managing it. It is important to ensure all contract information is passed to the appropriate people to ensure the potential pitfalls are addressed.

BEWARE OF "CREEPING COMMITMENTS"

Acting on the results of the evaluation

The importance of evaluation in coaching links straight back to the themes of "Finding the Right Coach" and "Getting the Best Value" outlined in Chapters 3 and 4.

If coaching is treated more like the purchase of a business product with clear specifications and associated rigour, and the hidden costs of poor coaching practices are avoided, then real coaching value can be delivered and measured.

By evaluating coaching programmes, it is possible to gather information about when to use them, who to use them for and when to stop them.

When to stop using a coach

At the beginning of the coaching assignment it is easy for the client to be seduced by the "feel good factor" that is generally associated with a relationship where the individual is given the chance to express their feelings in a confidential and supportive environment. This reaction is natural, and a good sign of a developing coaching relationship.

However, it is important that this kind of "halo" effect doesn't mask an underlying lack of progress in helping with improvements against clear organisational objectives. This is where ongoing evaluation across all of Kirkpatrick's levels is important, because it can help prevent the client from becoming/growing dependent on the coach. The dangers of dependency are often highlighted, with the concern that some clients find it difficult to end the coaching relationship. Early identification of over-dependence as a potential issue is therefore important.

As we have said before, coaching is about more than just making someone feel good. If it is not delivering against clearly agreed objectives, then an assessment has to be made by either the client or the business sponsor and a decision made to stop the coaching or look for another supplier/coach.

Contrary to the "touchy-feely" image of coaching often assumed by line managers, many organisations are adopting sound coaching practices and are using coaching to address significant business issues such as driving performance improvements and productivity.

 78% of respondents in the CIPD 2004 survey, reported using coaching for "improving individual performance"

30% use coaching for "dealing with underperformance"

20% for "improving productivity"

Coaching in a business context is about improving productivity and organisations in the future will be focusing much more on this aspect. Coaches who do not come up to scratch and are not delivering value should simply not have their contracts renewed.

CHAPTER SUMMARY

✓ Evaluating Coaching is about assessing it as a business tool.

✓ Success could be as simple as even bothering to do an evaluation at all.

✓ The Kirkpatrick model is helpful in providing a systematic evaluation tool.

✓ Simple standard feedback sheets based on the original contract criteria can provide good evaluation data.

✓ The intangible benefits should be recognised and included in the evaluation.

✓ Move beyond the individual benefit to measuring organisational benefits.

✓ It is possible and important to use an ROI process.

✓ Share the evaluation results and act on them (reward effective coaches and stop using less effective ones).

Chapter 7 – Looking to the future of coaching

It is clear that coaching through the 1990s and 2000s has seen exponential growth. It has become one of those "hot" areas of personal, professional and business development. From all evidence it is here to stay. It seems to fit well into the complex structures which make up most modern organisations. Coaching can adapt and cope with the rapid changes in business environments and support individuals through those changes. Within the wider social trend of personalisation, it was perhaps inevitable that personal and professional development would evolve to a one-to-one service. As the next generation of managers develop, their expectations will drive the demand for more one-to-one management development. Just as they require a personal fitness coach, and financial advisers on tap, so they will see the need for coaching to be provided in a bespoke way.

However, coaching is no longer a new concept and as people and organisations learn to use its benefits better (as prescribed throughout this book), then it is likely to evolve into an even more sophisticated and tangible business tool.

So what might "more sophisticated coaching" look like in the future and how might the benefits be quickly leveraged in an organisation?

This chapter looks at:

- Emerging themes
- Multilevel systems coaching
- Organisational Development (OD) coaching
- Professionalisation and specialisation
- The coaching organisation
- Coaching as leadership development
- Fusion coaching

Emerging themes

As a tool for individual development, coaching fits well with other processes such as personal development planning, 360 degree feedback, career planning and supporting leadership development in general. More specifically, and alongside other leadership processes, coaching can be aimed at improving leadership effectiveness at an individual level.

However, if coaching is used as one of the tools or processes in a larger change or transformation agenda, then the purpose of coaching will reinforce that agenda within a specific business context and with specific predetermined business goals. It will also help achieve improvements at the organisational level.

The concept of using coaching as an integrated part of a business transformation is an emerging theme. This is particularly true in organisations where coaching has become a more mature concept. This theme shows up under a number of different guises including some considered below.

1. Multilevel systems coaching
Multilevel systems coaching is about expanding a coaching intervention to include simultaneous coaching of individuals and groups within an organisation in order to create a shared learning at both the individual and organisational level. It has its roots in Organisational Development as much as coaching and combines the two disciplines for maximum organisational impact.

An Organisational Development consultant, who also works as an executive coach, has a perspective on both the way the organisation works (the system) and the individual. It is often the case that in a coaching setting, working with any one individual will not take account of the larger system that may be actually creating the set of behaviours (good or bad) that are exhibited by an individual.

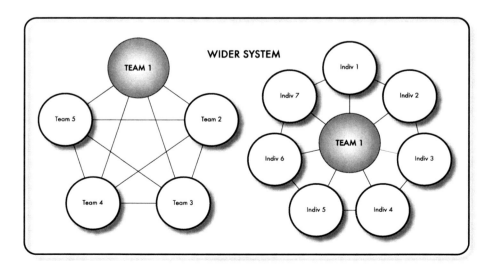

Figure 12. *Inter-relationship/layers in multi level coaching*

This is where "systemic" coaching is seen to add value.

"Systemic coaching is similar to individual coaching in that it focuses on accountability, ownership and impact on results. However, the difference is that it is multilevel and takes place with several individuals and groups at different levels simultaneously throughout the organisation." – Lisa Murrell et al 2006 from MetaSystem Consulting Group.

Systemic coaching provides both the individual and the group the chance to explore how their behaviour and actions impact the way the organisation (the system) works. We will see evidence of coaches who have clients throughout an organisation and can therefore provide a system wide view. In larger firms suppliers will provide a team of coaches, who combine their experience to get this view.

"When coaching is done in a systemic context, the feedback from those in the system is a more rich and powerful source of data to determine the direction of change than just dealing with the individual, or even the individual and their direct boss. Change and progress are much more profound when there is peer input and subsequent support." – Roland Sullivan, Co-Author of *Practising Organisation Development: A Guide for Consultants*.

2. Organisational Development (OD) coaching

Related to multilevel systems coaching is the concept of OD coaching. There are many similarities and links between OD and coaching. An underpinning link is that they both focus on change.

The distinction usually made between the two is that OD looks at the larger system and coaching looks at the individual. However, it is pretty much universally accepted that organisational change requires changes at the individual level. Often OD consultants will work with change leaders, stressing the importance of the leadership role in achieving and sustaining teams. In fact they are actually coaching them at the individual level to facilitate organisational change. But, it is not always the case that a coach will know the organisational context when working with an individual.

A trend going forward, therefore, is likely to be the powerful combination of the two fields of coaching and OD.

Perhaps the next 10 years will see the emergence of the OD coach where the disciplines become integrated in a specialist area with consequential benefits for both the individual and the organisation.

3. Professionalisation and specialisation

As the supply side of the coaching market grows and competition intensifies, there will be a strong driver for coaches to achieve recognised qualifications and specialise in niche areas. When we looked at where to find the right coach in chapter 3, we noted that the industry of training coaches was expanding.

"Training is essential in order to understand how to implement the core principles of coaching.

As well as the excellent schemes run by the three international bodies: Association of Coaching; International Coaching Federation and EMCC, some private training schools run their own assessment and accreditation programmes for students they have trained." – Carol Wilson, Best Practice in Performance Coaching. 2007.

These may be for particular client groups such as newly promoted managers, or CEOs or in particular areas of need such as Communication Skills or Personal Effectiveness. The Systemic Coach or OD Coach will be examples of such special coaches.

4. The coaching organisation

Peter Senge, author of the book *The Fifth Discipline: The Art and Practice of the Learning Organization*, has clearly established the case for the importance of a systems approach to creating and sustaining organisational change.

An emerging theme with similarities in the world of coaching is the creation of "The Coaching Organisation". The parallel to the learning organisation, is that it would see coaching as part of an overall system to the point where it becomes an embedded part of the organisational culture.

Creating a coaching organisation requires a commitment to and investment in a focused and integrated approach. A coaching organisation is underpinned by a coaching climate.

So what is a coaching climate? David Clutterbuck (2004) says that *"you will know you have a coaching climate when:*

➡ *Personal growth, team development and organisational learning are integrated and the links clearly understood*

➡ *People are able to engage in constructive and positive confrontation*

➡ *People welcome feedback (even at the top) and actively seek it*

➡ *Coaching is seen as a joint responsibility of managers and their direct reports*

> *There is good understanding at all levels about what effective developers and developees do*

> *Coaching is seen by managers as an opportunity rather than a remedial intervention*

> *People are recognized and rewarded for sharing knowledge*

> *Time for reflection is valued*

> *There are effective mechanisms for identifying and addressing barriers to learning*

> *People look first inside their organisation for their next job (typically only one in five do)*

> *There are strong role models for good coaching practice"*

So the concept of the coaching organisation certainly seems like a vision for the future and already some organisations are well down this track.

The BBC is one of them.

Case study

Liz Macann is the Head of Executive Leadership and Management Coaching at the BBC. Since 2001 she has been leading the way to create an internal coaching resource within the BBC. The desired objective is to "offer professional and executive coaching to all leaders and managers to a standard equal to or better than that which is available from external suppliers".

The "Coaching Network" that has been created has two full time Executive Coaches and a Project Manager. They deliver and manage a comprehensive programme which includes a rigorous selection process for the coaches supported by coach facilitation skills training, a systematic coach Continuous Professional Development (CPD) programme and monthly supervision sessions. At the end of 2007 they had 60 trained coaches, 12 trainee coaches and 10 supervisors. Internal Accreditation is optional, rigorous and externally moderated. Most coaches have achieved or are working towards this.

In a typical year the Coaching Network delivers/participates in:

> 500 coaching programmes

> 48 shared learning groups

➡ 12 CPD workshops

➡ 2 coach foundation skills courses (Executive Coach Training)

➡ 12 coaching skills for managers courses

➡ 12 industry speaking engagements

Individuals who received coaching as a component of the BBC's leadership programme were asked to rate its impact:

➡ 92% said they had increased confidence

➡ 95% felt they were better at managing performance

➡ 91% said coaching had helped them manage upwards

➡ 93% reported improvements in their development of strategy

Typical comments from executives who were recipients of the internal coaching support included:

"Very thought provoking. Each session was intellectually stimulating and quite demanding."

"It helped me to diagnose the issues, to articulate the key challenges, to prioritise where I needed to put my attention and come up with a realistic action plan."

"Coaching is like a mind gym, hard work but very refreshing."

It looks like the Coaching Network is well on the way to achieving the desired outcome of high and professional standards of coaching to all leaders and managers and the BBC has set the bar very high for internal coaching for other organisations.

Creating a coaching organisation is not easy, and requires a single-mindedness and much more concentrated approach than most organisations are prepared to consider. Again, David Clutterbuck tells us, based on two decades of research, that "for real change to happen, managers need a progressive level of skills improvement, easily accessed sources of advice, pressure from clients, positive role models and a supportive environment."

The approach takes us back to chapter 3 where we looked at the pros and cons of internal versus external coaching. In the case of the "coaching organisation" it becomes not the choice of one or the other but rather a coordinated and integrated use of both.

This of course, all comes at a cost. However, this cost may be less or at least a more effective investment than continually training and retraining managers with little impact over time.

 Key fact

In a study by Olivero, Bane and Kopelman (1997) they found that one-on-one executive coaching increased productivity by 80% compared to the effects of conventional management training alone (22.4%).

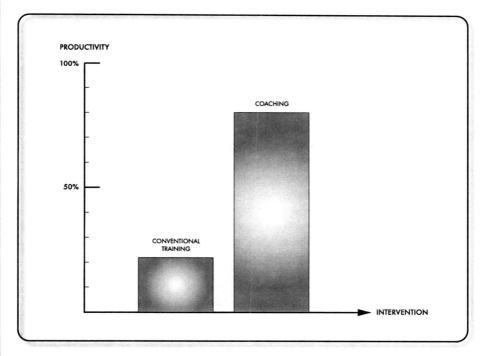

5. Coaching as leadership development

It could be said that the growth of coaching is a consequence of a greatly increased focus on leadership development by most forward-looking organisations. The link between strong leaders and strong business performance is well accepted and has led to a greater investment in leadership development. If coaching is also identified as part of the leadership development strategy, then long-term improvements measured by increased profit and decreased cost are the likely outcomes.

Strategic preparation for a coaching initiative, as part of the leadership development programme, starts with creating an awareness of the organisation's current critical success factors and their desired future position. Without a focus on organisational strategy then leadership development activity is likely to fail. Coaching can play a vital role in consistently reminding a leadership team of the key current and changing organisational priorities.

Another critical factor in leadership development is gaining clarity on the underpinning competitiveness needed to sustain the organisation through change. The best competency models blend organisational needs and individual leadership capabilities to form a list of desirable leadership behaviours, characteristics and skills.

As a result, competency models can provide an ongoing assessment tool in leadership development. If coaching is used to support a clear competency framework by reminding individuals and encouraging them to improve against their competency gaps, then the payback for the organisation can be very significant indeed.

Executive time is a scarce and valuable resource. It is unlikely to become less scarce in the future. As a result, senior leaders tend to shun formal leadership development opportunities. With a choice of an important leadership meeting, a global conference call, a presentation to stakeholders, or a set of numbers to be analysed, then the chances are that a leadership development experience will drop off their list (or at best be tolerated as a distraction in a busy world of e-mails). Coaching is key therefore as a leadership development tool in a world with time pressures. It is powerful, because used correctly it provides quick, effective and focused development.

In a coaching environment an executive will be able to set specific and measurable goals. The coaching environment promotes new behaviours, skill acquisition and practice. As a result, as a leadership development investment, the payback is more obvious, more bespoke and more relevant to the organisational objectives. The future, therefore, for successful delivery of leadership development programmes is intrinsically linked to combining this with well-structured coaching support.

6. Fusion Coaching

This final emerging theme is an attempt by the authors to pull together all the other emerging themes, and to build on some of the basic assumptions and good coaching practice discussed throughout the book. Just like the trend for "Fusion cooking" which blends different styles of cuisine from across the world then "Fusion Coaching" is about blending the best from individual and organisational styles of coaching to the benefit of both.

Basically a fusion coaching approach is about seeing and using coaching as a system intervention. It is based on the major assumption that all behaviour is context dependent. No behaviour is intrinsically good or bad, simply appropriate or inappropriate depending on the environmental/cultural context.

HAVE YOU EVER THOUGHT THAT HIS BEHAVIOUR IS NOT SO MUCH INTRINSICALLY BAD – BUT JUST *INAPPROPRIATE..?*

Coaching should help individuals by showing them how to read the environment and how to achieve organisational objectives.

Coaching in an organisational context can provide the ***individual*** with:

- The space to explore their understanding of organisational reality

- A chance to identify how organisational change might impact on their role

- An opportunity to identify positive personal and professional consequences of change

- An opportunity for rigorous support and challenging feedback on ways of thinking and behaving in a new context

- A safe environment for individuals to express their feelings and explore new possibilities in a positive way

Coaching in an organisational context can provide the ***organisation*** with:

- A support mechanism to enrol and encourage the players to participate in organisational change

> ➡ A consistent and measurable way of checking how individuals are responding to change

> ➡ A space where leaders are given a place to reflect on how they can adapt to a changed set of circumstances

In other words, to consider the joint benefits for the individual and the organisation, fusion coaching has to be about ensuring that coaching is part of a larger initiative and is systemic. It has to be used as part of an overall set of change interventions; it will be built into best OD practice in an organisation and will be an integral part of supportive leadership development programmes.

One additional suggestion as a powerful future use of coaching in an integrated way is the concept of using learning and insights from the coaching intervention for the organisation as a whole. In turn, this allows for organisational learning and maybe even strategic change as a consequence of that learning. This aspect of coaching has probably the greatest potential for delivering organisational learning, but there are very few organisations in the UK where coaching has reached this level of maturity.

 Case study

GSK is one of the few leading the field in having a coaching methodology that integrates most of the best elements.

In a global role covering pharmaceutical manufacturing involving some 34,000 employees across 80 countries, Sally Bonneywell, Vice President, L&OD, is clear that coaching makes a significant difference when targeted at the leadership population. The emphasis is on internalising coaching capability and the creation of a coaching organisation. The aim is to embed coaching as a leadership competency so that successful leaders are inherently good coaches. This is in turn supported by high quality external coaching. Coaches are carefully screened by interviews, which check for sound experience, recognised qualifications and good references. Most importantly they are tested through a trial coaching session. Leaders are offered four names of the screened coaches and allowed to make a choice based on personal chemistry fit.

Once on board the screened and tested coaches are brought together in a group twice a year to collect, in confidence, the key organisational themes and learning points that can be used to inform future organisational strategy.

This is about coaching that combines improvement in leadership performance with organisational learning, which is potentially a very powerful approach.

The demand for coaching has been growing over the last five years and this integrated approach is helping to meet it effectively and efficiently.

This model of coaching ticks almost all of the boxes and offers a best in class example of what the authors mean by "fusion coaching".

Asking Sally Bonneywell the difficult question of "What is missing?", she replies honestly: "The quest for finding a good measure of the ROI for coaching remains the Holy Grail. At present it remains mostly anecdotal and it would be great to have a clearly articulated business case, which shows the return on the investment. We all know it is there, it would just be nice to show it clearly."

It sounds like GSK will "crack this nut". Meanwhile they exhibit all the elements of best practice coaching and provide an excellent role model.

Fusion coaching involves gathering organisational learning by setting up learning cells with preferred suppliers of coaching. The learning cells will meet regularly (probably quarterly) to review the individual and organisational trends, changes of business direction and for experiences to be shared in order to learn from each other. Involving a mix of both internal and external coaches adds to the richness of the potential benefits and helps raise standards and levels of competence across the whole coaching population. It also helps to ensure that the learning and intellectual property associated with that learning stays in the organisation.

As in the case study, for a fusion approach to coaching to work well it needs all the principles of good coaching practice to be working in perfect harmony, as described throughout this book. An important element is a disciplined approach to buying coaching. In other words, it requires:

- Clear definition of requirements
- Well articulated needs analysis
- Accurate specifications
- Sound procurement
- Measurement of results

➡ Setting of targets

➡ Checking of references

➡ Robust feedback

If all these are in place (and of course the personal chemistry works!), then the way is set for real added value to both the individual and the organisation. A possible flowchart diagram of how this might work in practice is illustrated below:

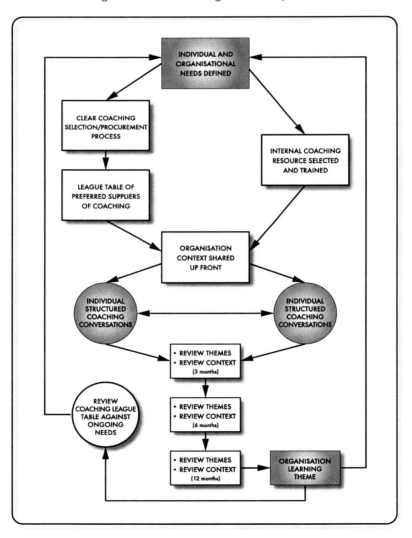

Figure 13. *Fusion coaching approach*

This diagram describes the perfect world of coaching and no organisation will conform exactly to this model. However, it sets the direction for what might be possible in the future. It also comes with its own pitfalls, and some of these are highlighted below:

Pitfalls

➡ Care must be taken in using data from coaching interventions to inform wider dialogue about the organisation, so that appropriate levels of confidentiality are maintained and the individual coaching contract is not broken

➡ Coaching can often yield a vast amount of information that may previously have been unavailable to those heading up a change initiative. This information should only be used when informing and improving leadership interventions, and not as an instrument of social control

➡ There must be an acute awareness of boundary issues, always remembering who is to be served by the coaching interventions (individual, organisation, sponsoring client, other stakeholders)

Confidentiality

Among the most sensitive of these pitfalls is confidentiality. Trust is a critical component of a successful coaching relationship. However coaches and organisations alike can often offer inappropriate promises of full confidentiality to the clients. Business coaching within an organisation is typically not bound by the same conditions of confidentiality that can be found in life coaching (when the coaching is paid for by the individual) or in a clinic/patient relationship (i.e. those that occur in clinical practice or in Employee Assistance Programme relationships with companies.)

The importance of the original contracting conversation is key to this if organisational issues are to be drawn from a conversation without breaking basic trust. Negotiated levels of confidentiality, where parameters for handling the information by both coaches and participants are clearly set out and agreed prior to the coaching assignment, will help ensure trust and thus more effective outcomes. Discussion and agreement on how records will be kept, what will be put in writing and who owns the data are very important at an early stage.

In summary, a fusion approach to coaching will be sensitive to the needs of all stakeholders, respecting the relationship positions and be of benefit to all. These different fields of application are shown in Figure 15.

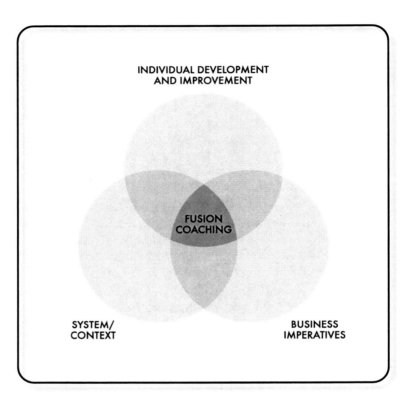

Figure 14. *Fields of application of fusion coaching*

Perhaps the last words are best left to the well known coach, Myles Downey (Effective Coaching, Myles Downey, 2003), who says:

"Coaching brings more humanity to the workplace. Effective coaching in the workplace delivered achievement, fulfilment and joy in which both individual and the organisation benefit."

CHAPTER SUMMARY

✓ There are a number of emerging themes which indicate the future for coaching.

✓ Multilevel coaching works at both the individual and organisational level.

✓ Organisational Development coaching starts to combine two very compatible disciplines to maximum effect and gives coaching an organisational context.

✓ "The Coaching Organisation" can be said to emerge when coaching becomes embedded in the culture of the organisation.

✓ Coaching can be used very effectively alongside and in combination with Leadership Development activities.

✓ A model for a fully integrated "fusion" approach to coaching, which feeds back learning into the organisation is potentially a very significant future development.

✓ There are pitfalls to be aware of and it is always important to and build trust consider confidentiality in the coaching relationship.

Bibliography

CIPD (2007). CIPD Guide, "CIPD Learning and Development Survey".

Clutterbuck, D (2003). *Creating a Coaching Climate*. Clutterbuck Associates.

Clutterbuck, D. and Megginson, D. (2004). *Techniques for Coaching and Mentoring*. Butterworth-Heinemann.

Dembkowski, S., Eldridge, F. and Hunter, I. (2006). *The Seven Steps of Executive Coaching*. Thorogood.

Downey, M. (2003). *Effective Coaching: Lessons from the Coaches Coach*. Texere.

Gray, D. (March 2005). "Principles and Processes of Coaching Evaluation", *EMCC Journal*.

Jarvis, J. (2004). *Coaching and Buying Coaching Services*. CIPD, 2004.

Johnson, L.K. (2007). *Getting More from Executive Coaching*. Harvard Management Update.

Kirkpatrick, D.L. (1996). *Evaluating Training Programs: The Four Levels*. Berrett-Koehler.

Kolb, D.A. and Fry, R. (1975) "Toward An Applied Theory of Experiential Learning", in C. Cooper (ed.) *Theories of Group Process*. John Wiley.

Michelman, P. (2005). "Do You Need An Executive Coach?", Harvard Management Update: Article U0412D.

Olivero, G., Bane, K.D., Kopelman, R.E. (1997). "Executive Coaching as a Transfer of Training Tool: Effects on Productivity in a Public Agency", *Public Personnel Management Journal*, Vol. 26.

Parsloe, E. (1999). *The Manager as Coach and Mentor*. IPD.

Pedler, M., Burgoyne, J. and Boydel, T. (1996). *The Learning Company*. McGraw-Hill.

Phillips, J. and Stone, R. (2002). *How to Measure Training Results: A Practical Guide to Tracking the Six Key Indicators*. McGraw-Hill

QED Consulting Survey, (June 2006) "More Spend, More Coaching: Trends In Training And Management Development".

Senge, P.M. (1992) *The Fifth Discipline*. London: Nicholas Brealey Publishing Ltd.

Senge, P.M (1994) *The Fifth Discipline Field Book*. London: Nicholas Brealey Publishing Ltd.

Sherman, S. and Freas, A. (2004) "The Wild West of Executive Coaching", *Harvard Business Review*.

Sullivan, R. and Rothwell, W.J. (1995) *Practicing Organization Development: A Guide for Consultants*. Pfeiffer & Company.

Whitmore, J. (2002) *Coaching for Performance; Growing People, Performance and Purpose*. Nicholas Brealey Publishing Ltd.

Wilson, C. (2007) *Best Practice in Performance Coaching*. Kogan Page.

Zenger, J.H. and Stinnett, K. (July 2006) "Leadership Coaching: Developing Effective Executives". *Chief Learning Officer Magazine*. Media Tec Publishing.

About the authors

Clare Moore runs the coaching and consultancy firm, Business Jigsaw. An effective and experienced business coach, she is able to draw on 15 years of management experience at British Airways and Telewest Broadband.

Clare moved into the business coaching area after taking part in a leadership programme, which involved using a coach. She was a stressed-out senior manager with a very young family, and used the opportunity of the coaching sessions to design a new lifestyle. This involved moving to a different part of the country and starting up her own business, initially in consultancy. The firm has grown strongly since 2003 and the team of coaches at Business Jigsaw now work with managers in the private and public sector.

More information on the services offered by Business Jigsaw can be found at www.businessjigsaw.com

Brian Wishart runs his own HR consultancy business, Wishart Consultancy, which specialises in executive coaching, leadership development and organisational design. With over 20 years experience as an HR Director with BP he has a practical and hands on approach to providing coaching solutions for senior executives. Previously Head of Learning for BP in Europe he was accountable for the purchasing and supply of external coaching. He has used the learning from this along with a breadth of experience in the private, public and voluntary sectors to provide tried and tested methods for getting the most from an investment in coaching.

Brian moved into formal coaching following a career where he found coaching to be fundamental in helping others succeed in their chosen field of work. He uses a variety of approaches based on the client's need but specialises in executive coaching or in career management coaching where individuals may feel "stuck" in their current role.

More information on the services offered by Wishart Consultancy can be found at www.wishartconsultancy.co.uk

Tools and resources

The following documents are also available to download from our website at www.buyersguidetobusinesscoaching.com

➡ Definition of Coaching Terms

➡ Request For Information Checklist

➡ Template Request For Information Form

➡ Request for Information Cover Letter Template

➡ A Selection of Coaching Training Providers

➡ Am I Ready For A Business Coach – Questionnaire

➡ Learning Style Diagnostics (Honey and Mumford)

➡ Code of Ethics and Good Practice, Association for Coaching

Definition of coaching terms

The definitions of coaching terms used in this book and included in the diagram in Chapter 2 are taken from the CIPD definitions provided in their *Coaching and Buying Services Guide* (2005).

These are given below for reference:

Performance coaching. Coaching activities here are aimed at enhancing an individual's performance in their current role at work. The specific issues covered by the coaching will vary, but the aim will always be to increase their effectiveness and productivity at work. Generally, performance coaching derives its theoretical underpinnings and models from business and sports psychology as well as general psychological theory.

Skills coaching. This form of coaching focuses on the core skills an employee needs to perform in their role. Skills coaching provides a flexible, adaptive, 'just-in-time' approach to skills development. Coaching programmes are tailored specifically to the individual and are generally focused on achieving a number of skill development objectives that are linked to the needs of the organisation.

Career coaching. Coaching activities focus on the individual's career concerns, with the coach eliciting and using feedback on the individual's capabilities as part of a discussion of career options. The process should lead to increased clarity, personal change and forward action.

Personal or life coaching. This form of coaching provides support to individuals wishing to make some form of significant change happen within their lives. Coaches help individuals to explore what they want in life and how they might achieve their aspirations and fulfil their needs. Personal/life coaching generally takes the individual's agenda as its starting point.

Business coaching. Business coaching is always conducted within the constraints placed on the individual or group by the organisational context. The term is used to refer to any coaching activity that takes place in a business setting, so by definition overlaps with other terms.

Executive coaching. Organisations are now generally more willing to invest in coaching for their senior managers and executives. By improving the performance of the most influential people within the organisation, the theory goes that business results should improve. Executive coaching is often delivered by coaches operating from outside the organisation whose services are requested for an agreed duration or number of coaching sessions.

For further information contact:

CIPD, 151 The Broadway, London SW19 1JQ, UK
www.cipd.co.uk

Request for information checklist

What should be included in an RFI process depends on the specific needs of both the individual and the organisation, but some of the key questions that should be considered would include:

➡ What is the track record of the individual/consultancy?

➡ Where have they worked before?

➡ Are there references available?

➡ What is their organisational bench strength? Do they have a "first" and "second" team and how do you ensure you get the first team?

➡ Do they have the resources to cope with the size of the project?

➡ What is their specific understanding as to the scope of the work and how aligned is this with the intent of the client/organisation?

➡ What steps will the coach take to avoid "scope-creep" and what overview will the organisation have?

➡ What does final/complete delivery look like?

➡ Will they build capacity into the organisation and what tools do they have to demonstrate capability in this area?

➡ What tools do they have to identify best practice?

➡ What performance management model do they prefer to use in working with clients to ensure that improved performance can be tracked?

➡ What internal processes do they have to manage their own staff?

➡ How do they provide assurance for the client on confidentiality?

➡ What will they do if confronted with really difficult issues like stress, ethical or legal challenges?

➡ What is their position on sharing tools with other consultancies/the host client?

➡ What is their track record of coaching culturally diverse clients?

➡ What do they cost?

➡ How do they charge?

➡ Are they themselves professionally supervised and do they provide supervision arrangements for coaches under their control?

➡ What are their relevant qualifications and most recent training?

➡ Are they members of professional bodies and are they relevant?

➡ Do they hold professional indemnity assurance?

Template request for information [RFI] form

Coach Information Sheet

Please be aware of the completion notes at the bottom of the information sheet, which offer clarifying details on how to complete this profile.

1	Name	
2	Main existing company x contact[1]	
3	Internal/external references[2]	x references: • Name – Job Title – Email • Name – Job Title – Email • Name – Job Title – Email Outside references • Name – Job Title – Email • Name – Job Title – Email • Name – Job Title – Email
4	Contact details	Email Phone(s) Website(s) Mail address Fax Best way to contact me
5	Preferred coaching style[3]	
6	Main coaching expertise	Development: yes/no Performance: yes/no Improvement, transition, or transformation Individual, team, or system
7	Other lines of business[4]	
8	Level(s) of leadership coached	Team leaders Senior leaders Executive leaders

9	Worked in specific parts of *x*, or specific industry/ies	Business unit: Function: Strategic performance unit: Segment: Region: Industry:
10	Description of 3 of your coaching interventions from the last 3 years. What did you do? What was successful? Please describe generically to avoid issues of confidentiality	
11	Fee structure[5]	Hourly rate: Daily rate: Coaching package rate:
12	Relevant training and thinking paradigm[6]	
13	Accreditation[7]	
14	Inter cultural capabilities[8]	
15	Language(s) capabilities[9]	
16	Use of technology for coaching[10]	Phone, email, video, eLearning, interactive (e.g. netmeeting and phone)
17	i. On average, how long did your coaching interventions take? ii. What do you find to be the minimum time required to see any progress in a client coaching relationship? iii. How do you evaluate the need to continue the relationship with your client?	

| 18 | i. State the techniques you use to assess progress towards objectives set in the contracting stage?
ii. How do you ensure that this is done rigorously? |
| 19 | How have you been building coaching capability in client organisations? |

Completion notes

[1] Your main contact will be accountable for managing the relationship between you and *x*. This would include keeping your individual information up to date and keeping an evaluation track of the coaching you would undertake in *x*. For suppliers who have never worked in *x*, please note NA.

[2] 6 names are required. 3 from *x*, 3 from outside. Include at least 4 colleagues (i.e. beyond HR).

[3] We are aware that the most skilful coaches do adapt their style to the situation. So specify which is your preferred style, not the style(s) you can display.

[4] E.g. counsellor, trainer, mentor, expert consultant.

[5] Specify either the fixed rate or the range, depending on your current way of charging for a coaching intervention.

[6] Detail which coaching programmes you have been through and what certifications you have gained. Please indicate also from which school(s) of thought you draw your coaching philosophy, and what are your relationships to these schools (e.g. attended a training; part of a consortium; on-going partnership with the school of thought).

[7] Have you been accredited by a coaching body? If yes, which body is this, in which country, and what was the accreditation process? If not, what other ways do you use to demonstrate your ethical and professional standards?

[8] Specify from which culture(s) you would feel able to provide insights and challenges to a client. Which cultures have you experienced enough that you consider yourself as an advocate of them?

[9] Specify in which languages you could deliver coaching, underlying the languages in which you have already performed coaching in the past.

[10] Beyond face-to-face, how do you deliver coaching?

Request for information cover letter template

Dear

We would like to invite you to take part in a process to become an accredited supplier to *x* for the provision of individual coaching services.

A number of documents are attached to this letter, which give further details and set out the Request for Information (RFI), which we invite you to complete.

We would also like to provide some background to explain why we are launching this piece of work.

As you know, the HR function within *x* is committed to delivering both appropriate quality and value for money services to its business clients. We are therefore creating a database of companies and individuals who can provide this high quality of service.

We are therefore asking recognised coaching providers to follow our Procurement Process. This is a two part process, with the RFI being followed by a Request for Quotation (RFQ). The RFQ will be an open competitive market process.

Your responses to the RFI will form an integral part of the data used in the selection process, which will lead to a limited pool of eligible vendors who will receive a Request for Quotation.

In order to ensure that you have completed everything fully, we have offered guidance within the questionnaire that you should read carefully.

We request that you complete the attached RFI in full. It consists of Company Questions and a Coach Information Sheet.

The Company Questions are about your company and need only be completed once. The Coach Information Sheet is about each individual coach. As we will be accrediting individual coaches rather than companies, we would be grateful if you would ensure that each individual in your consultancy – who you wish to be considered as a potential coach completes the Coach Information Sheet.

Those accredited as suppliers of Coaching Services to *x* will become part of a recommended list of providers.

Please submit 2 A4 copies in a sealed envelope and a virus-checked copy on either Microsoft Excel or Microsoft Word, sent by e-mail. The hardcopy should be marked RFI HR ref:xxx for the attention of _____. It should arrive no later than Noon on _____.

> The information contained in this and other documents, or as a result of subsequent discussions, is to be treated in the strictest confidence.
>
> Receipt of this RFI in no circumstances whatsoever implies the existence of a commitment or contract by or with x for any purpose.

To ensure that the process is fair and that all providers are treated ethically and equally, ALL clarification should be directed *by fax or e-mail* to:

Name

e-mail

Fax

This will enable us to offer generic clarifying email responses to all participants.

Please acknowledge receipt of this RFI and confirm your intention to participate in providing the information requested, in order to be considered for any future RFQ for Individual Coaching Services.

Thank you for your time and attention,

A selection of coaching training providers

Association of Coaching accredited training providers

The Beech Consultancy www.thebeechconsultancy.co.uk

The Centre for Coaching www.centreforcoaching.com

The Executive Coaching Consultancy Ltd www.executive-coaching.co.uk

Penna www.e-penna.com

Performance Coach Training www.performancecoachtraining.com

Spark www.sparkcoachingandtraining.org

Pharos www.pharosperformance.co.uk

The Performance Solution www.theperformancesolution.com

OPM www.opm.co.uk

The Grove Practice Ltd www.counselling.org

Acorn Principle Plus Ltd (APP Ltd) www.theacornprinciple.com

UK College of Personal Development www.ukcpd.net

EMCC quality approved training providers

Name of company	Name of programme	Award category
CIPD	Certificate in Coaching and Mentoring	Intermediate
	Advanced Certificate in Coaching and Mentoring	Practitioner
Contact: Adele Smith, CIPD, 151 The Broadway, London SW19 1JQ URL: http://www.cipd.co.uk/CMSTraining/Coaching/Coaching.htm		
The Chief Executives' Office	Executive Business Coach Programme (Modules 1–3)	Intermediate
	Post Graduate Certificate in Executive Business Coach Programme (Modules 1–4)	Practitioner
Contact: John Webster, The Chief Executives' Office, Aston Hall, Aston-on-Trent, Derbyshire DE72 2DE Email: ceo@ceogb.co.uk		
Clutterbuck Associates	Foundation programme	Conditional. Quality Award in the Foundation category
Contact: David Clutterbuck, Clutterbuck Associates, Grenville Court, Britwell Road, Burnham, Bucks SL1 8DF Email: david@clutterbuckassociates.co.uk		

| Management Futures | Coaching Programme – Modules One and Two | Practitioner |

Contact: Alan Rogers, Executive Director, Management Futures Ltd, 37 Grays Inn Road, London WC1X 8PQ
Email: alan.rogers@managementfutures.co.uk

Oxford School of Coaching and Mentoring	Certificate in Coaching for Performance	Foundation
	Diploma in Professional Coaching and Mentoring	Intermediate
	Advanced Diploma in Professional Coaching and Mentoring	Practitioner

Contact: Eric Parsloe O.S.C.M, Centrepoint, Chapel Square, Deddington, Oxford OX15 0SG
Email: eric@oscm.co.uk
URL: http://www.oscm.co.uk/index.html

| Oxford Brookes | MA Coaching and Mentoring Practice | Master |

Contact: Dr Elaine Cox, Oxford Brookes University, Westminster Institute of Education, Harcourt Hill Campus, Oxford OX2 9AT
Email: ecox@brookes.ac.uk
URL: http://www.brookes.ac.uk/schools/education/macoachment.html

| PB Coaching | Fundamentals of Coaching Programme | Conditional. Quality Award in the Foundation category |
| | Intermediate Coach training Programme | Conditional. Quality Award in the Foundation category |

Contact: Peter Bluckert Coaching, 12B Russell Court, Woolgate, Cottingley Business Park, Bingley BD16 1PE
Email: mail@pbcoaching.com

PDF/Middlesex University	Practitioner course	Practitioner
	MA/MSc in Professional Development	Master
	Master Coach Designate	Master

Contact: Dr David Lane, 21 Limehouse Cut, 46 Morris Road, London E14 6NQ
Email: david.lane@pdf.net

| Praesta Partners LLP | Practitioner programme | Conditional. Quality Award in the Practitioner category |

Contact: Robin Linnecar, Praesta Partners LLP, 83 Pall Mall, London SW1Y 5ES
Email: robin.linnecar@praesta.com

Sheffield Hallam University	Post Graduate Certificate in Mentoring and Coaching	Practitioner
	Post Graduate Diploma in Mentoring and Coaching	Advanced Practitioner
	MSc in Mentoring and Coaching	Master
Contact: Paul Stokes, Sheffield Hallam University, School of Business and Finance, Stoddart Building – City Campus, Howard Street, Sheffield S1 1WB		
Email: p.k.stokes@shu.ac.uk		
Tavistock Consultancy	Executive Coaching Skills	Intermediate
Contact: Judith Bell, Tavistock Consultancy Service, 120 Belsize Lane, London NW3 5BA		
Academy of Executive Coaching	Foundation Programme	Intermediate
	Advanced Diploma Programme	Practitioner
Contact: Sue Pegg, Academy of Executive Coaching Ltd, 64 Warwick Road, St Albans, Herts AL1 4DL		
Email: training@aoec.com		
URL: http://www.aoec.com		

ICF accredited training

http://www.coachfederation.org.uk/icf_accredited_training.phtml

Coaching & Mentoring Network's training directory

http://www.coachingnetwork.org.uk/resourcecentre/TrainingAndAccreditation/

Am I ready for a business coach – questionnaire

Questionnaire for potential coaching client	Tick
I am willing to take responsibility for improving my performance	
I have a clear purpose and motivation to change	
The issues I want to work on are mainly job related rather than personal	
My improvement needs are about skills and knowledge at work rather than any medical conditions	
I trust that the conversations I might have with a coach will be confidential	
I am willing to open up to a coach, sharing personal information and being very honest	
I am prepared to commit to spending regular time with a coach	
I am prepared to commit to specific goals and outcomes	

Learning style diagnostics (Honey and Mumford)

The Learning Series and the work of Dr Peter Honey

In a world where the rate of change is increasing and where international competition is more intense, learning is the only competence that never becomes obsolete. Continuous learning is, quite simply, the key to sustained innovation and competitiveness.

Written by Dr Peter Honey, The Learning Series is a suite of self-assessment online questionnaires dedicated to helping people become better all-round learners.

It does this by overhauling people's learning processes and is unique in taking such a hard, helpful look at how people learn. This benefits individuals by increasing their willingness and ability to learn from formal and informal opportunities.

It benefits organisations by having people who adapt better to change, learn faster than competitors and take responsibility for their own development.

The online questionnaires that make up the Learning Series are:

- **Learning Needs Analysis Questionnaire**
- **Learning Styles Questionnaire (40-item or 80-item)**
- **Learning Motivation Questionnaire**
- **Learner's Environment Questionnaire**
- **Manager's Environment Questionnaire**
- **Learning Skills Questionnaire**

The Learning Series gives learners immediate results and tailor-made suggestions for action. Users can also develop personal development plans.

The Learning Series combines the reliability and quality of Peter Honey's work with the many benefits of electronic learning.

For further information please contact:

Peter Honey Publications Ltd
10 Linden Avenue
Maidenhead
Berkshire
SL6 6HB

Tel: 01628 633 946
Fax: 01628 633 262
Email: info@peterhoney.com
Web: www.peterhoney.com

Code of ethics and good practice – Association for Coaching

The Association for Coaching is committed to maintaining good practice. This Code of Ethics and Good Practice sets out the essential elements of sound ethical practice. For the purposes of this code, the person receiving coaching is called the client.

All Clients should expect a high standard of practice from their Coach. To ensure that this is achieved coaches commit to operate in accordance with the Association's Code of Ethics and Good Practice for ethical, competent and effective practice.

1. Coaches are required to recognise both personal and professional limitations:

    Personal – with respect to maintaining their own good health and fitness to practice. Should this not be the case, coaches are required to withdraw from their practice until such time as they are in good health and fit to resume. Clients should be offered appropriate, alternative support during any such period.

    Professional – with respect to whether their experience is appropriate to meet the client's requirements. When this is not the case, clients should be referred to other appropriate services, e.g. more experienced coaches, counsellors, psychotherapists or other specialist services. In particular, coaches are required to be sensitive to the possibility that some clients will require more psychological support than is normally available within the coaching remit. In these cases, referral should be made to an appropriate source of care, e.g. the client's GP, a counsellor or psychotherapist, psychological support services and/or agencies.

2. Coaches are responsible for ensuring that clients are fully informed of the coaching contract, terms and conditions, prior to or at the initial session. These matters include confidentiality, sessional costs, and frequency of sessions. All claims made by the coach should be honest, accurate and consistent with maintaining the coaching profession's good standing.

3. Coaches are required to be frank and willing to respond to their client's requests for information about the methods, techniques and ways in which the coaching process will be conducted. This should be done both prior to contract agreement and during the full term of the contract.

4. Coaches must be sensitive to issues of culture, religion, gender and race.

5. Coaches must respect the client's right to terminate coaching at any point during the coaching process.

6. Coaches are required to maintain appropriate records of their work with clients, ensuring that any such records are accurate and that reasonable security precautions are taken to protect against third party disclosure. Attention must be given to the coachee's rights under any current legislation, e.g. data protection act.

7. Coaches are required to monitor the quality of their work and to seek feedback wherever possible from clients and other professionals as appropriate.

8. Coaches are expected to have regular consultative support for their work.

9. A coach should aim to undertake a minimum of 30 hours of continuing professional development in the theory and practice of coaching on an annual basis.

10. Coaches are required to keep themselves informed of any statutory or legal requirements that may affect their work.

11. Coaches are required to have current professional liability insurance.

12. Coaches are required to consider the impact of any dual relationships they may hold with regards to their clients and/or any sponsoring organisations.

13. Coaches must act in a manner that does not bring the profession of coaching into disrepute.

Printed in the United Kingdom
by Lightning Source UK Ltd.
130501UK00001B/595-669/P